James Joyce and the Philosophers at Finnegans Wake

James Joyce and the Philosophers at Finnegans Wake

Donald Phillip Verene

NORTHWESTERN UNIVERSITY PRESS
EVANSTON, ILLINOIS

Northwestern University Press
www.nupress.northwestern.edu

Printed in the United States of America

10 9 8 7 6 5 4 3 2 1

Library of Congress Cataloging-in-Publication Data

Names: Verene, Donald Phillip, 1937– author.
Title: James Joyce and the philosophers at Finnegans wake / Donald Phillip Verene.
Description: Evanston, Illinois : Northwestern University Press, 2016. Includes bibliographical references and index.
Identifiers: LCCN 2015047125| ISBN 9780810133310 (pbk. : alk. paper) | ISBN 9780810133327 (cloth : alk. paper) | ISBN 9780810133334 (e-book)
Subjects: LCSH: Joyce, James, 1882–1941. Finnegans wake. | Joyce, James, 1882–1941—Criticism and interpretation. | Bruno, Giordano, 1548–1600—Influence. | Nicholas, of Cusa, Cardinal, 1401–1464—Influence. | Vico, Giambattista, 1668–1744—Influence.
Classification: LCC PR6019.O9 F59386 2016 | DDC 823.912—dc23
LC record available at http://lccn.loc.gov/2015047125

Tutto, tutto, tutto è memoria.
Everything, everything, everything is memory.

—Giuseppe Ungaretti

CONTENTS

PREFACE

Finnegans Wake was published in 1939, an advance copy of which arrived in James Joyce's hands in Paris on January 30, a few days before his fifty-seventh birthday. Two years later, on January 13, 1941, Joyce died in Zurich, having left the uncertainties of Unoccupied France for the safety of Switzerland. Joyce formed the first thoughts of what was to become *Finnegans Wake* shortly after the appearance of *Ulysses* in 1922. He developed this new work under the title *Work in Progress*, publishing parts of it in periodicals, principally in issues of *transition*, founded and edited by his longtime friends Eugene and Maria Jolas.

When *Finnegans Wake* appeared in copies for sale in May 1939—published simultaneously in London and New York—Joyce had been famous for years as the author of *Ulysses*, with a readership that was beginning to understand his work, and a critical literature that was building upon it. *Finnegans Wake* appeared, to the reading public and to critics alike, as unreadable, even unapproachable, except perhaps as a literary curiosity. Joyce found the reviews few and disappointing.

In 1944 Joseph Campbell and Henry Morton Robinson, in *A Skeleton Key to Finnegans Wake*, the first book to interpret the *Wake*, reported that "the public reception was one of massive indifference. 'What does it all mean?' 'Why should we bother about a book so hard to read?' were questions quite generally asked. Even normally responsive readers dismissed the book as a perverse triumph of the unintelligible." Ezra Pound, Joyce's longtime critic and supporter, put it this way in 1926, in responding to the typescript Joyce sent him of the Shaun book of *Work in Progress*: "Nothing so far as I make out, nothing short of divine vision or a new cure for the clap can possibly be worth all the circumambient peripherization."

The emphasis on *Ulysses* as Joyce's master work has persisted as generations have learned to read it. No more evidence of this orientation is needed than to look into Gordon Bowker's *James Joyce: A New Biography* (2011), a work intended for general readers. We learn of all aspects of *Ulysses* and Joyce's work leading up to it, but *Finnegans Wake* struggles for a full place in its pages. More recently, the novelist and physician Rivka Galchen, in a "Bookends" column for the *New York Times Book Review* of February 2, 2014, marking both Joyce's birthday and the one-hundredth anniversary of the serialization of *A Portrait of the Artist as a Young Man*, remarked that "Joyce wrote poems, a play, a terminally perfect collection of short stories, a terminally perfect künstlerroman, a nearly terminally perfect 'Ulysses,' and then that other book, the one supposedly published in English but written in no language anyone fully understands." She continues: "Occasionally we come across people claiming to have read all of 'Finnegans Wake,' but one hears them as if listening to a rashy traveler returned feverish from distant jungles, telling of a city built entirely of gold."

In his note to the new edition of *Finnegans Wake* (see the "Bibliographical Note" on page xix herein), Seamus Deane says: "There has always been a large majority of readers for whom *Finnegans Wake* is, as part of its rationale, unreadable; indeed, unreadability has always been part of its attraction, the pseudo-suave explanation for never having read it. That view of, approach to and refusal of the work are all now outdated."

Richard Ellmann, in his definitive biography, *James Joyce*, reports that Nora Joyce, living on in Zurich after her husband's death, was distressed by the disregard of Joyce's last book. She asked Maria Jolas: "What's all this talk about *Ulysses*? *Finnegans Wake* is the important book. When are you and Eugene going to write about it?" Although Nora once said she did not read any of her husband's books, and thus did not concern herself much with them, she was right about *Finnegans Wake*. Joyce spent a third of his life producing it. It supersedes *Ulysses*, as Joyce intended. Without question, *Ulysses* and *A Portrait* are great works in their own right. But as the first two works of Joyce's trilogy, with *Dubliners* as the introduction, they take the reader to *Finnegans Wake*, just as they took Joyce.

The reader of Joyce who decides to press on, to attempt to enter Joyce's "nightmaze" (411.08) rather than turn back to extol the merits of Bloom's day in *Ulysses*, must find a way to cross the threshold. Two ways are possible. One way, that taken by most interpreters, is simply to begin reading, to identify the central characters and seek out the story line, much in the way one would approach any modern novel. On this approach, *Finnegans Wake* poses special problems only because the story must be seen through the complexities of Joyce's language, which must be surmounted to some extent along the way. The second way is to heed the advice Joyce consistently gave—to all his friends, to his benefactor Harriet Shaw Weaver, and to others who wished to know how to approach *Work in Progress* as it developed—to read Vico's *Scienza nuova*. Those who did not read Italian he referred to Michelet's French translation, as no English edition existed at that time.

Vico's work, which Joyce discussed as early as 1911 to 1913 at Trieste with his pupil Paolo Cuzzi in his English-language lessons and perhaps read even earlier, in whole or part, during his university studies in Dublin, contains the structure upon which *Finnegans Wake* was built. As Anthony Burgess remarked in his introduction to *A Shorter Finnegans Wake*: "What Joyce found in Vico was what every novelist needs when planning a long book—a scaffolding, a backbone." It is necessary, for the interpretation of *Finnegans Wake*, to grasp the story and many of Joyce's puns and references. But to do so is still only to float on its surface and not to approach the depth of its meaning. The reader needs to penetrate the intellectual structure out of which it is formed. The problem of its depth is not solved by the few pages of observations regarding Vico's *New Science*—that Joyce adapts a version of Vico's cycles and is influenced by Vico's conception of etymology—that one finds in the critical literature on *Finnegans Wake*. Joyce knew Vico well; his reader needs to, too.

The reader must read the two books together—*Finnegans Wake* and the *New Science*—as a "twone." Such reading requires "two thinks at a time." Each book will change in the reader's mind in relation to the other. As Joyce restudied Vico's *Scienza nuova* to write *Finnegans Wake*, as Ellmann reports, the reader can be expected by Joyce to do the same. Most readers will likely be led to study Vico for the first time. Joyce's text, more than any other in the twentieth century, more than Croce's work, has pointed to the originality and wealth of insights that lie within the *New Science*. Joyce is in fact Vico's greatest interpreter, although his purpose was not to be an interpreter in any ordinary sense.

Many critics have associated Joyce's writing with stream of consciousness, a term coined by William James in *Principles of Psychology*, and in a wider sense also associated with psychoanalysis. Joyce, however, claimed his technique was one of interior monologue, the source of which was his encounter with Édouard Dujardin's novel *Les Lauriers sont coupés*. Dujardin claimed the starting point for the soliloquy of the novel was the philosopher Fichte's dialectical conception of the I as opposing itself to the not-I. Joyce put aside any debt to psychoanalysis in his remark to the Danish novelist Tom Kristensen, on advising him to read the *Scienza nuova* to understand *Work in Progress*. Joyce said: "My imagination grows when I read Vico as it doesn't when I read Freud or Jung." In a conversation Joyce had in the 1930s with the Zurich publisher Daniel Brody regarding Jung's negative assessment of *Ulysses*, he said: "People want to put me out of the church to which I don't belong. I have nothing to do with psychoanalysis." In the *Wake* we find: "when they were yung and easily freudened, in the penumbra of the procuring room and what oracular comepression we have had apply to them!"—one of a number of unflattering and comic passages on the founders of psychoanalysis.

The Neapolitan, Giambattista Vico (1668–1744), arrives at the *Wake* in its first sentence "by a commodious vicus of recirculation" (see the comment on "commodious" in the "Bibliographical Note" herein). A paragraph later appears the first of Joyce's ten Vichian thunder words, the longest words in the English language. In Vico's *New Science* the clap of thunder is the primordial appearance of Jove, causing the offspring of the sons of Noah—who have grown to the size of giants, wandering the great forest of the earth after the universal flood—to flee into caves, to form marriages and found families, thus beginning the gentile nations of the great city of the human race. In the marginalia of the classbook section in the middle of the *Wake* appears a list of each of Vico's major ideas, beginning with "IMAGINABLE ITINERARY THROUGH THE PARTICULAR UNIVERSAL," the "imaginative universal" (*universale fantastico*) that Vico says is the "master key" to his work.

The fourth and last part of the *Wake* reminds the reader of its principle of "Our wholemole millwheeling vicociclometer" that operates by Joyce's fourfold transformation of Vico's three ages of "ideal eternal history" (*storia ideale eterna*), described in various combinations of four terms, here as "eggburst, eggblend, eggburial and hatch-as-hatch can." And the *Wake* gives the final instruction, "mememormee!"—echoing Vico's claim, to which Joyce subscribed, that "memory is imagination" (*la memoria è la stessa che la fantasia*).

Joyce's other philosopher, practitioner of the art of memory, and advocate of the coincidence of opposites (*coincidentia oppositorum*), Giordano Bruno (1548–1600), arrives at the *Wake* with Vico, with whom he is recirculated. A commode or chamber pot is a Jordan, Bruno's first name in English. A Jordan is originally a bottle of water brought from the Jordan River by Crusaders or pilgrims. Vico is connected to the Jordan River by his first name, Giambattista (Giovanni Battista), which in English is John the Baptist, the saint who preached and baptized along the Jordan. Vico, born on June 23, was baptized on June 24, the day of Saint John the Baptist. Bruno is the accused heretic, "the Nolan," born at Nola near Naples, part of the Comune di Napoli, who, refusing to recant, was burned at the stake by the Inquisition in the Campo de' Fiori at Rome on February 17, 1600.

In the Latin passage of the classbook section of the *Wake* we find "*Jordani et Jambaptistae mentibus revolvamus sapientiam*," Joyce recirculating the letters of the two philosophers' first names, corresponding to the letters of his own name. When Joyce writes: from "a jambebatiste to a brulobrulo!" we hear the sound of the burning faggots in the play on Bruno's name. In the millwheeling vicociclometer passage, Bruno's doctrine of opposites appears as "the dialytically separated elements of precedent decomposition for the verypetpurpose of subsequent recombination," thus joined with Vico's cyclic conception of history.

Joyce embraces these two philosophic companions as his guides through the underworld of history with all its repetitions and resurrections that run through its oppositions and recombinations. We as philosophical readers of the *Wake* go along with them to meet everybody and in so doing "to encounter for the millionth time the reality of experience and forge in the smithy" of our souls the "uncreated conscience" of our race. In Joyce's use of "conscience" we encounter Vico's "*conscientia*"—the recognition of what we find but do not create. Philosophical readers who are accustomed to seek the clarity and distinctness with which Descartes founds modern philosophy are invited by Joyce to enter his book of the dark and see what is on the other side of Descartes's brightly lit room, warmed by the heat radiating from his *poêle*.

How are we to read *Finnegans Wake*, a book that, once opened, forces us immediately to reconsider all we have ever learned about the art of reading? Joyce's book redefines what it means to read. Joyce once suggested that it be regarded as a language, and Beckett, in his famous *Exagmination* essay, written with the hand of Joyce close by, concludes that Joyce—like Dante, who created an Italian that had never been spoken to write the *Divine Comedy*—created an English in which the words used to speak about a thing become the thing itself, what today in philosophical terms can be called "performative utterances," in which what is said does not refer to some separate act that is described, but is the act itself.

As is well known, a great writer does not leave the language in which he writes his work the same as it was when he came to it. It is no more possible to steal a line of Shakespeare than to steal the club of Hercules or a line of Joyce. Joyce alters not only the English language; he alters what language itself is. "Are we speachin d'anglas landadge or are you sprakin sea Djoytsch?" As litter becomes letter we encounter at Joyce's hands a new sense of what literature is. Language is taken back to its original power to make and remake the world—the power previously reserved to the mythic word.

I first read *Finnegans Wake* while living for a year in Florence, a copy borrowed from the British Institute Library. I had nothing more in mind than approaching a large and complicated book that would fill in some time when not working on the book on Vico I was writing. The connection between Joyce and Vico was not my purpose. Like many other readers of books, for me *Finnegans Wake* was simply a book that for a long time I had intended to read. The year was 1980 and the residents of Florence still kept to the order of their day that it seemed had not changed since Galileo and Machiavelli lived there. At one o'clock all shops and offices closed for their occupants to return home for *pranzo*, the major meal of the day. Following the meal, like most of the city I took my *pisolino*, a little nap, before resuming work in the long Italian afternoon.

Each day I read a page or more of the *Wake* before drifting into sleep, to "A scene at sight. Or dreamoneire. Which they shall memorise," only to awake and repeat the process for many months until I arrived at "A way a lone a last a loved a long the." During the mornings and afternoons I coursed and recoursed Vico's science of imagination and in between coursed Joyce's imagination, with no more purpose than moving from page to page, scene to scene, listening in semiconsciousness in my mind's ear to the words. I became somewhat "earsighted."

A second event that concerned reading *Finnegans Wake* occurred five years later, in the summer of 1985, in connection with a conference, held at the Princess Grace Memorial Irish Library at Monaco, regarding the issue of the original 1922 edition of *Ulysses* versus the new 1984 Gabler edition. The conference involved what Anthony Burgess called a "*Finnegans Wake* approach to *Ulysses*," meaning that Dublin offers a specific reference point for the contents of *Ulysses*, but *Finnegans Wake* can only be approached as a text. The Gabler edition takes a purely textual approach to the meaning of *Ulysses*. In a plenary session Fritz Senn, founder and director of the James Joyce Foundation in Zurich, who was a member of the session panel, pointed out that no one actually reads *Ulysses* in the 1922 edition, and suddenly asked the audience, a large number of Joyce scholars from various countries, who among them had in fact read *Finnegans Wake*.

Before what I thought would be a unanimous show of hands, I asked if he intended "read" in any particular sense. Senn replied, "No, just having gone through the pages." Sitting in the front row, raising my hand, I turned around to see—at least in my line of vision—no other raised hands, in what was an awkward moment of silence. A further question was raised: whether anyone would say what he or she thought the book was about. Hearing no response, I said I thought it to be a book of wisdom, and that a book of wisdom was one that contained, in principle and to an extent in fact, all that there is, a truth of the whole. No one remarked further on this.

Much later that evening, while sitting in the lobby of the Hôtel de Paris Monte-Carlo with Richard Ellmann, the great Joyce biographer, who was then my colleague at Emory University, and chatting while watching the hotel guests returning from the casino nearby, I asked Dick to explain the events at the panel. Why, in a room of Joyce scholars, would no one publicly acknowledge having read the *Wake*, and why, having read it or not, no one would venture an opinion as to how it may be approached or regarded. As a philosopher I was unaccustomed to such reluctance to express one's views. Ellmann explained that no one responded for fear of jeopardizing their professional reputation. As generally an outsider and a literary amateur, whatever I said or did was of no matter. I found myself in a most auspicious place, and still do. The freedom to say what one thinks is of the greatest value. As Cicero claimed, the arts, as liberal arts, are based on freedom.

Joyce said he had done enough to keep the critics busy for a long time—and he had. Ellmann was an exception. Without his monumental biography the whole of Joyce would not be present for us. My first memory of this mild-mannered scholar was a lunch together in a café in Emory Village, where he immediately placed an order for a whiskey "with lots of ice" and a bowl of chili "with lots of chopped raw onions on top." To my mind it trumped Bloom's deliberation at "Davy Byrne's. Moral pub." resulting in a good glass of Burgundy and slender strips of a gorgonzola sandwich.

Ellmann's approach to the meaning of Joyce's text could be quite direct. He was to introduce a lecture that Derrida was giving at Emory on the final "Yes." of *Ulysses*, and he asked me if I had any advice, as I was to do the same the following day for Derrida's lecture on Heidegger. I said I had no special advice except I understood that Derrida tends to speak at length. Dick said: "I think I'll take half the time and give him the other half," an unusual decision for someone whose duty was simply to chair the session.

He introduced Derrida by citing the ancient description of Pythagoras—that he was world famous and had a golden thigh—and then said: "That Derrida is world famous is beyond doubt, that he has a golden thigh remains to be seen." Following this Dick explained to the large audience exactly what the "Yes" meant in *Ulysses*. It is a word intended to be beyond all context or classification or analysis, a cosmic affirmation (in other words, it was a word when so used that stood beyond any grammatology, any doctrine of deconstruction). Then he turned the remainder of the session over to Derrida, to read his complicated paper. Ellmann's introduction of Derrida was a surprise for me, equaling that of his lunch order. The content of his remarks gave me a lasting sense of how Joyce could be spoken of in a direct and absolute way.

My reading in Florence and my collegial friendship with Ellmann has been my particular route to the *Wake*. They are circumstances that forced Joyce on me and led finally to the chapters that follow. Each reader must find a way to cross the threshold of the work and find a place at the *Wake*. In so reading the *Wake*, whether we think we comprehend it or not, our best method is just to keep reading, to move along with the riverrun of the pages. And when this is done, I think, the reader will find that he or she has been there already, all along.

To interpret Joyce's work, more is required than to read it. Reflecting on meeting Joyce for the first time, at a session of the P.E.N. Club, the French critic Louis Gillet wrote to Paul Valéry that "it was an evening that made one long to speak every language, and I hear that in order to appreciate *Finnegans Wake* one really ought to know seventeen." Roland McHugh, in his *Annotations to Finnegans Wake*, employs sixty-two abbreviations for various languages and dialects in the text. In addition, there are instances of, for example, Maori and Estonian.

To read *Finnegans Wake*, and to have something scholarly to say about it, I think, the reader should know, in addition to English and Latin, the languages of the three Continental countries in which Joyce lived—Italy, Switzerland, and France. He spoke fluent Italian, German, and French. It is not enough to consult dictionaries of these languages and Latin to understand what Joyce writes. These are the languages that, more than others, flow throughout the text. The interpreter of Joyce's work needs to be able to go along with Joyce's use of them with ease. English and a smattering of these three are not enough. Gillet's estimate of what is required is extreme, but the more languages one knows would be, of course, all to the good. Joyce also spoke Danish.

Beyond the language requirement, Joyce can expect his best readers to have an extensive knowledge of history, including that of Ireland and Scandinavia, and of the great books of the world, ancient, modern, East, and West. *Finnegans Wake* is as close to a complete speech of humane letters as can be found and, perhaps, ever will be found.

I wish to acknowledge my debt to the *Finnegans Wake* reading group, who met for many years on Wednesday afternoons, in the Library of the Institute for Vico Studies at Emory University, to compare views on a randomly chosen page of the work. I never left a session without hearing and seeing the page differently, if not also seeing the world somewhat differently. It was a gathering of intellects, a series of precious moments.

My thanks to Alex Léon for our conversation one afternoon in 2010, at my home in Atlanta, concerning his boyhood memories of James Joyce in Paris in the 1930s, when his father, Paul Léon, acted as Joyce's secretary and managed his literary affairs. They met daily at the Léon residence. Alex is likely the only one alive today who had personal contact with Joyce.

My thanks to my colleagues at Emory and elsewhere who saw this work in manuscript: Raymond Barfield, Thora Ilin Bayer, Ann Hartle, Benjamin Kleindorfer, Donald Livingston, David Lovekin, Frederick Marcus, and William Willeford.

My greatest thanks to Molly Black Verene, who transcribed my handwritten sheets into typescript, while raising valuable questions and suggestions, without which this work would not have come to life.

BIBLIOGRAPHICAL NOTE

The edition of *Finnegans Wake* employed herein is the original published by Faber and Faber, London, 1939, cited by page and line, a copy of which I purchased in Dublin in 1995. I have also consulted the critically emended edition edited by Danis Rose and John O'Hanlon, published by Houyhnhnm Press (Dolphins, The Parade, Mousehole, Cornwall, England, 2010). In quotations, except in a few instances, I have kept to the 1939 edition, the text to which most readers have reprint access. An exception to be noted here, because it concerns the introduction of Vico's name in the first sentence of the *Wake*, is that the critical edition corrects "commodius" of the 1939 edition to its dictionary spelling of "commodious." I have followed the critical edition in this instance.

The editors of the 2010 edition state: "The new text differs from the old in about 9000 instances. This sounds grander than it is. *Finnegans Wake* comprises some 220,000 words, or about six times that number of characters, letters, spaces and punctuation marks. . . . Overwhelmingly, the changes pertain to the syntax (the flow of the words) rather than to the semantics (their individual meanings)." My concern in this study is semantic rather than syntactic. For the reader who is reading the *Wake* as a whole, the syntax is important for grasping the musical quality of the text, as the editors indicate.

The English translation of the *New Science* employed herein is that of Thomas Goddard Bergin and Max Harold Fisch, revised and unabridged, published by Cornell University Press (Ithaca, N.Y., 1984), cited by the paragraph enumeration. The Italian edition employed is the original as anastatically reprinted: *Principj di Scienza nuova d'intorno alla comune delle nazioni* (Naples, 1744), edited by Marco Veneziani, published by Olschki, Florence, 1994. I have also consulted the recent critical edition *La Scienza nuova 1744*, edited by Paolo Cristofolini and Manuela Sanna, vol. 9, *Opere di Giambattista Vico* (Rome: Storia e Letteratura, 2013).

The critical literature on both Joyce and Vico is very large. A place to start on Joyce are the bibliographies in A. Nicholas Fargnoli and Michael P. Gillespie, *James Joyce A to Z: The Essential Reference to the Life and Work* (Oxford: Oxford University Press, 1996), appendix VI. A place to start on Vico is Molly Black Verene's bibliography, "Works on Giambattista Vico in English from 1884 through 2009," *New Vico Studies* 27

(2009): 83–304. For works in Italian and various languages see Benedetto Croce, *Bibliografia vichiana*, revised and expanded by Fausto Nicolini, 2 vols. (Naples: Ricciardi, 1947), and its supplements in the series "Studi vichiani," published by Guida for the Centro di studi vichiani, as well as the issues of its *Bollettino*, Naples.

As pointed out in the preface, few writers on Joyce give attention to Vico. An example of this lack of attention are the essays in *The Cambridge Companion to James Joyce*, edited by Derek Attridge (New York: Cambridge University Press, 1997), which contain only the slightest mentions of Vico (and only a few comments on Bruno, with no mention at all of Nicholas of Cusa). A reader coming for the first time to the question of the relation of Joyce and Vico may turn to James S. Atherton's well-known *The Books at the Wake: A Study of Literary Allusions in James Joyce's Finnegans Wake* (Carbondale: Southern Illinois University Press, 2009; 1959), only to discover that it devotes but five pages to Vico and another two to Cusanus and Bruno, and that they appear as authors of structural books at the *Wake*, presented more or less equally with such little-known authors as Morton Prince and James Hogg.

The reader interested in Vico and wishing to go through *Finnegans Wake* section by section, from beginning to end, will find that William York Tindall's *A Reader's Guide to Finnegans Wake* (Syracuse, N.Y.: Syracuse University Press, 1969) consistently and usefully calls attention to places where Vico (as well as Bruno and Cusanus) appears in the *Wake*. Hugh Kenner's remarks on Vico's sense of language and use of etymology in chapter 18 of his *Dublin's Joyce* (New York: Columbia University Press, 1987; 1956) is very much worth attention, as is the third chapter on *Finnegans Wake* in Umberto Eco's *The Aesthetics of Chaosmos: The Middle Ages of James Joyce* (Cambridge, Mass.: Harvard University Press, 1989).

The major exception to the general lack of detailed discussion of Vico in the critical literature on *Finnegans Wake* is John Bishop's admirable study, *Joyce's Book of the Dark: Finnegans Wake* (Madison: University of Wisconsin Press, 1986), which contains a chapter on "Vico's 'Night of Darkness': The *New Science* and *Finnegans Wake*."

I am pleased to note that the spelling of "*Ricorso*" (instead of "Recorso") as the title of book 4 of Joseph Campbell and Henry Morton Robinson, *A Skeleton Key to Finnegans Wake*, has been corrected in its new edition, edited by Edmund L. Epstein (Novato, Calif.: New World Library, 2005; 1944). It is notable that this first book-length examination of *Finnegans Wake* acknowledged throughout the connections of Joyce's work to the *New Science*. Readers may wish to look at Norman

O. Brown's curious *Closing Time* (New York: Vintage, 1973), the text of which consists largely of juxtapositions of passages from Vico and Joyce.

Vico studies have given limited attention to Joyce and Vico. Two early essays are of particular note: A. Walton Litz, "Vico and Joyce," in *Giambattista Vico: An International Symposium*, edited by Giorgio Tagliacozzo and Hayden V. White (Baltimore: Johns Hopkins University Press, 1969), 245–55; and Stuart Hampshire, "Joyce and Vico: The Middle Way," in *Giambattista Vico's Science of Humanity*, edited by Giorgio Tagliacozzo and Donald Phillip Verene (Baltimore: Johns Hopkins University Press, 1976), 321–32. A justification for Joyce not having been a specialist topic in Vico studies is that Vico scholars are not required to relate Vico to Joyce in order to interpret Vico, even though there is benefit in so doing. Joyce scholars, however, need to understand Vico, since Joyce himself instructed all to do so in regard to *Finnegans Wake*.

It is unlikely that anyone can truly be expert equally on both Joyce and Vico. Having been drawn from Vico to Joyce and back, my own previous attempts to provide the "two thinks at a time" that are needed to connect them have been twofold. My first attempt was to organize a weeklong international conference in Venice in 1985 that resulted in my edited volume of seventeen essays, *Vico and Joyce* (Albany: State University of New York Press, 1987), that begins with an essay on *Finnegans Wake* by Northrop Frye and contains a mixture of essays by Joyce and Vico scholars. My second attempt was my *Knowledge of Things Human and Divine: Vico's New Science and Finnegans Wake* (New Haven, Conn.: Yale University Press, 2003), which took up the theme of Joyce as the major twentieth-century interpreter of Vico. My claim was not that Joyce's purpose was to interpret Vico but that we might take this approach as a way to comprehend Vico.

Three reference works are essential for the study of *Finnegans Wake*. Clive Hart, *A Concordance to Finnegans Wake*, corrected edition (Mamaroneck, N.Y.: Paul P. Appel, 1974; 1963); Adaline Glasheen, *Third Census of "Finnegans Wake": An Index of the Characters and Their Roles* (Berkeley: University of California Press, 1977); and Roland McHugh, *Annotations to Finnegans Wake*, revised edition (Baltimore: Johns Hopkins University Press, 1991; 1980).

James Joyce and the Philosophers at Finnegans Wake

Introduction

✦

Plato's Ancient Quarrel

Plato's Poets

The locus classicus for consideration of the connection between philosophy and poetry is the tenth book of the *Republic*, in which Plato takes up for the second time the place of poetry in human education and human knowledge. Earlier, Socrates has established that while poetry may provide us with pleasure, it is unable to provide us with moral principles and thus be a guide to the just and good life. Poetry can affect the psyche but it does so indiscriminately, for in it both good and bad actions of people and gods are portrayed with equal validity. Thus, Socrates says, "we'll say that what both poets and prose writers [*logopoioi*, makers of speeches] say concerning the most important things about human beings is bad."[1] All literary expression is defective in this way: "Of poetry and tale-telling, one kind proceeds wholly by imitation [*mimēsis*]—as you say, tragedy and comedy; another, by the poet's own report—this of course, you would find especially in dithyrambs; and still another by both—this is found in epic poetry and many other places too."[2]

Because of this failure of poetry to embody principles whereby we may distinguish good from bad, just from unjust, it is defective in its content. Furthermore, it is defective in its form, whether it is declaimed by rhapsodes or recited as lines by actors in comedies or tragedies. Both rhapsodes and actors imitate good and bad persons and actions with equanimity. Thus those who interpret literary productions for us simply follow and portray the moral oscillations present in them. Socrates finally says: "Now, as it seems, if a man who is able by wisdom to become every sort of thing and to imitate all things should come to our city wishing to make a display of himself and his poems, we would fall on our knees before him as a man sacred, wonderful, and pleasing." But Socrates adds, "we would say that there is no such man among us in the city, nor is it lawful for such a man to be born there."

In the city in speech that Socrates is forming for us it would be against the divine order for such a poet to develop. He could appear only as a self-invited guest who would think himself well received. But Socrates says: "We would send him to another city, with myrrh poured over his head and crowned with wool."[3] The poet, thinking himself a great success, even a celebrity in the Socratic city, would unexpectedly find himself honored by being sent on his way. While accepting praise and adulation, he would find himself outside the gates of the philosophically ordered city.

As a young man in Dublin in 1902, Joyce expressed the view that he distrusted Plato. At the same time he also professed no interest in Homer, holding that the Greek epics and Hellenism are outside the tradition of European culture, and claiming that Dante's *Divine Comedy* was Europe's epic.[4] He did not hold to this early view, given the presence of Daedalus as the background of *A Portrait* and the ports of call of Odysseus as the sequence of *Ulysses*. Joyce, with his great interest in and facility for languages, never studied classical Greek but instead, as he states, studied Italian.[5]

His view of the separation of Hellenistic and European culture is Vichian, whether at that time he intended it or not. Vico's conception of Western history is that the ancient world constitutes a *corso* in which Homer is the summary figure of the first two ages of Greek gods and heroes, the third age of distinctively human law and intellect arriving with Socrates and the philosophers. European culture is a *ricorso*, with Dante occupying a place analogous to Homer, such that Vico calls Dante the "Tuscan Homer." Dante summarizes the medieval world and is followed by the Humanist philosophers of the Renaissance and, later, by the Cartesians and the modern conceptions of law and society of the seventeenth-century natural-law theorists, led by Grotius and Hobbes. On Vico's philosophy of history there is no continuous development from the ancient world to the modern; the modern only recapitulates the ancient in different terms.

Did Joyce put aside his early distrust of Plato? This distrust may have been based on Plato's treatment of the poets: whether Plato would replace poetry with philosophy. In the Scylla and Charybdis episode of *Ulysses*, in the exchange between Stephen and Eglinton over the arts and the merits of Plato and Aristotle, is: "John Eglinton, frowning, said, waxing wroth:—Upon my word it makes my blood boil to hear anyone compare Aristotle with Plato.—Which of the two, Stephen asked, would have banished me from his commonwealth?"[6] In the fourth part of *Finnegans Wake* is the line: "How they housed to house you after the Platonic garlens" (622.35–36). The "Platonic garlens" crown the poet when he is ushered to the gates of the city, to be housed now not in the city but in the gardens outside the walls. In the tenth book of the *Republic* the condition is set for the reentry of the poets, but it is a condition that cannot be fulfilled simply in poetic terms: "let it be said that, if poetry directed to pleasure and imitation have any argument to give showing that they should be in a city with good laws, we should be delighted to receive them back from exile, since we are aware that we ourselves are charmed by them."[7]

Socrates says we have an inborn love of poetry, especially when we "contemplate it through the medium of Homer," and thus we would be glad if such an apology were possible and forthcoming by poetry. "But as long as it's not able to make its apology [defense speech], when we listen to it, we'll chant this argument we are making to ourselves as a countercharm, taking care against falling back again into this love, which is childish and belongs to the many [*hoi polloi*]."[8]

Joyce has a reference to Plato's quarrel: "hoping against hope all the while that, by the light of philophosy, (and may she never folsage us!) things will begin to clear up a bit one way or another within the next quarrel of an hour" (119.04–6). Plato says that even though we must "agree that Homer is the most poetic and first of the tragic poets" we cannot allow poetry in our perfect city. He says: "let it be our apology that it was then fitting for us to send poetry away from the city on account of its character. The argument determined us. Let us further say to it, lest it convict us for a certain harshness and rusticity, that there is an old quarrel between philosophy and poetry."[9] There is, in fact, not an old quarrel between philosophy and poetry, as it has only just been forged by Plato through Socrates's city in speech. But Plato says we will say it is old. With age comes reverence, and we will, he says, point to various signs that it is an old opposition based on lines from poets allegedly attacking philosophy. Plato proceeds to quote a few lines that he claims come from such poets.

Plato's quarrel with the poets involves not only the claim that poetry cannot supply principles of moral wisdom but also, as in the *Ion*, that the making of poetry requires a kind of madness on the part of the poets and the rhapsodes who recite it. It is the Muses who govern the poets, but, as Hesiod says, they told him "'we know how to tell many falsehoods that seem real: but we also know how to speak truth when we wish to.'"[10] For Plato the philosopher must intervene to move the speech of what may seem real to a speech of the truly real.

Joyce has put the Greek word for light in "philophosy"—*phōs*, the contraction of *phaos*. This philosophy is the love (*philia*) of light or clarity and a play on *filofol*, that suggests a "fine madness" or "*fine folie*," *fine* (Italian) also implying a final or ultimate kind of madness, a madness for clarity. "May she [philosophy] never folsage us!"—"*saige-fol*" (literally, "wise-crazy").[11] This is the Platonic clarity of the sun, identified with the Good that illuminates vision outside the dream-world of the images on the wall of the Platonic cave. Joyce has reversed the quarrel because the philosophers have their own kind of madness—their attachment to clarity. Here Plato's ideas (*eidē*) are joined with Descartes's famous clear and distinct ideas, his light of nature, or *clarté*.

In the episode of the Ondt and the Gracehoper, the Ondt is "swarming of himself in his sunnyroom, sated before his comfortumble phullup-suppy of a plate o'monkynous and a confucion of minthe (for he was a conformed aceticist and aristotaller)" (417.14–16). Here is Descartes again, with Plato. Descartes with his certainty, his clarity, of *cogito ergo sum*, seated in the warmth of his comfortable *poêle*, full of philosophy, and then Plato, with a plate of "monkynous" (monkey nuts, peanuts). As Joyce indicated in his letter to Harriet Shaw Weaver of March 26, 1928: "monkynous = monkey nuts also the 'nous' rational intelligence cf monasticism." Joyce also indicates: "confucion of minthe, confession of mind 'infusion de menthe,'" which connects with the asceticism and Aristotelianism of monasticism.[12] The Platonic *nous* requires us to climb up the tree of knowledge to the forms, which can only be reached by intellection, or *noēsis*, the top of the Divided Line. By contrast, a few lines earlier on the page: "The Gracehoper who, though blind as batflea, yet knew, not a leetle beetle, his good smetterling of entymology asped nissunitimost lous nor liceens but promptly tossed himself in the vico" (417.03–6).

The bottom of the Divided Line is the imagination, or *eikasia* of the poets, who know only images or *eikones*. *Poiein* is to make in general and in particular to compose poetry. The poets are makers through words. The words of the poets imitate things that are visible with the bodily eye. The philosophers are also makers through words, for example, makers of the city in speech. They are also imitators in this making, for their words lead us to, or make for us, a knowledge of the forms, which can be seen only with the mind's eye.

The quarrel with the poets, put in epistemological terms, is intense because the productions of the poets seem to take us to the nature of things. These productions do not merely mirror the visible world, they seem to take us into the very form or meaning of its visibility, such that we do not merely see things but see into things. Before it is given its Platonic sense, *eidos*, as it appears in Homer, means "what one sees," "appearance," "shape," usually of a body. For Plato the *eidē* exist in some intelligible place (*topos noetos*), just as the *aistheta*, or sensible phenomena, exist in the organic unity of the *kosmos*. In later Platonism they are located beyond the heavens in a *kosmos noetos*. The *eidē* are transcendent but they are immanent as well because things are claimed to participate (*methexis*) in the *eidē*. The philosopher can with words lead the "friends of the forms" to the noetic grasp of the real, to what we might call the "really real" (*to ontos on*).

In saying that the philosopher imitates the forms in language, I do not mean that there can be a literal statement of their nature. The philosopher's speech always points only to the nature of things. It never contains them. Plato makes this clear in the famous Seventh Letter, where he says: "there does not exist, nor will there ever exist, any treatise of mine dealing therewith. For it does not at all admit of verbal expressions like other studies, but, as a result of continued application to the subject itself and communications therewith, it is brought to birth in the soul on a sudden, as light that is kindled by a leaping spark, and thereafter it nourishes itself."[13] True philosophy is never written down, because it can never be written down.

Plato's doctrine of the ideas or forms is one of the most complex, difficult, and unresolved problems in philosophy. It is not my aim here to do full justice to it. My aim is only to suggest that the quarrel is based on the fact that poetry and philosophy are types of literature, the one a language of images and the other a language of ideas. Both are mimetic uses of language that differ in their objects of reference, the one visible and the other invisible. Images have no intrinsic standard either moralistic or epistemic, as an image can be made of anything good or bad, true or false. Ideas in our minds imitate the pure forms or *eidē* and are principles from which all else can be judged and known.

Plato's quarrel sets the agenda of Western philosophy—its chief problem is to forge a kind of thinking and language that separates it from poetry. To oppose a given philosophy on the grounds it is poetry is to condemn it immediately—a criticism from which no philosophy can ever recover. Plato leaves us in this position. We must choose Homer or Plato. In Homer's hands is the mantle of the music that gives pleasure to the *psychē*. In Plato's hands is the garland ready for use.

Vico's Fables

Joyce cannot trust Plato because of his willingness to limit poetry, to allow litter to become letter but not to allow letter fully to become literature. Although Joyce cannot trust the Platonism of Plato, he can trust the Neoplatonism of Vico. Vico's *New Science* is founded upon a resolution of the ancient quarrel between Plato and Homer. Indeed, as Vico holds, it is the master key to his science, the discovery of which, he says, cost him the greatest part of his intellectual life. One of the axioms of his science is that "doctrines must take their beginning from that of the matters of which they treat" (314). This, in fact, echoes a line in Plato's *Timaeus*, "Now in regard to every matter it is most important to begin at the natural beginning."[14]

This principle led Vico to the discovery "that the principle of these origins both of languages and letters lies in the fact that the first gentile peoples, by a demonstrated necessity of nature, were poets who spoke in poetic characters" (34). It also led him to the discovery that Homer was not a philosopher and should not be treated as such, as Plato did. For "by the very nature of poetry it is impossible for anyone to be at the same time a sublime poet and a sublime metaphysician, for metaphysics abstracts the mind from the senses, and the poetic faculty must submerge the whole mind in the senses, metaphysics soars up to universals and the poetic faculty must plunge deep into particulars" (821).

Vico offers a solution to the ancient quarrel so simple that we may wonder why it was not formulated earlier in the history of philosophy. He attributes wisdom to both poetry and philosophy but claims one wisdom, poetic wisdom (*sapienza poetica*), comes before the other. Poetic wisdom is found in fables and is the first form of human thought. Philosophy comes later, and the "intelligible universals" (*universali intelligibili*) or logical class concepts it employs presuppose "imaginative universals" (*universali fantastici*) that are embedded in poetic characters. The trope which governs poetic logic is metaphor and every metaphor is a fable in brief ("*ogni metafora sì fatta vien ed essere una picciola favoletta*") (404). What Vico calls poetic wisdom we would today call mythic thought, and, as Ernst Cassirer says, Vico "is the real discoverer of the myth."[15]

Mythic or poetic thought in this primordial sense does not attain to irony. Every fable is *vera narratio*, "true narration," just as every perception is true in itself. True and false perceptions enter the mind only through its attainment of the power of judgment, which becomes knowledge when incorporated in a rational account of what is originally perceived. The trope of irony enters the formation of human experience only with philosophical wisdom or reflective thought because irony "is fashioned of falsehood by dint of reflection which wears the mask of truth [*perch'ella è formata dal falso in forza d'una riflessione che prende maschera di verità*]" (408).

The language of intelligible universals is that of ordinary thinking as reflected in the logic of Aristotle. Particulars are grouped together in terms of their common properties and these species are organized into genera in a hierarchy culminating in ten categories or the most general predicates that can be attributed to a thing. Universals are thus abstracted from the particulars they originally order as *infima species*. An abstract property can be univocally predicated of individual entities which differ accidentally among themselves but manifest a common property. Thus a group of individuals who differ in their particularity, for example, can be said to share equally in the predicate "brave." This way of understanding the world is originally the product of philosophical reflection that becomes the way of common thinking.

The founders of the gentile nations, however, did not first think in these terms. Their minds were unable to form intelligible universals. Their minds, like the minds of children, excelled in imagination and imitation (215). They were also unable to form ironic speech, because irony requires a mentality that can distinguish true from false and speak the false as if it were true, thus asserting one thing while meaning another. The first human thoughts were governed not by rational reflection but by the poetic or mythic imagination or *fantasia*. The first human beings were poets who made their world through the power of metaphor. This original power of metaphor did not have the logic of putting the name of one thing in place of another, as Aristotle holds in his well-known claim in the *Poetics*. In this Aristotelian sense a metaphor is a compressed analogy through which one thing is seen as like another.

The first humans faced the problem of making things in the world out of the pure immediacy of perception, in which every physical sensation appears as a different being in an ongoing flow of sensations. These first humans "regarded every change of facial expression as a new face" (700). Vico's narration of the first human thought is that, after the universal flood, some of the offspring of the sons of Noah grew into giants, over two centuries, as the world dried out. They lost the religion of their father and the institutions upon which human society is based, especially marriage.

Wandering in the great forests of the earth, they encountered thunder and lightning as new phenomena, caused by the drying-out of the earth. They then felt fear for the first time, not fear of a specific danger but fear or terror (*spavento*) of being alive. They imitated the sound of thunder by uttering "*Pa!*" then doubling it as "*Pape!*" The first word they formed was the onomatopoetic sound of Jove, Jupiter Tonans (448). With this word they were able to grasp that each of the sensations of the incidences of thunder they felt were not appearances or perceptions of separate beings but that these particular thunders were all the presence of Jove.

Jove's body was the sky. This alter-body was divine, of an opposite order of being to their own. Their ingenuity (*ingegno*) did not rise to the level of abstracting similarity in the dissimilar, for each instance of thunder was at once a complete particular and a complete universal, a complete being of Jove. Jove was a particularized universal or, as Joyce puts it, theirs was an "IMAGINABLE ITINERARY THROUGH THE PARTICULAR UNIVERSAL" (260R3). Once one thing can be named, all can be named, and the world of flora and fauna becomes full of gods for them. The first humans thus entered Vico's first age of ideal eternal history—the age of gods. This original power of metaphor is the power of identity. It is an original metaphysics or theology, which elaborates the metaphorical identity into mythical narratives or fables that make the first truths of human experience.

As humanity develops in Vico's ideal eternal history from the age of gods to the age of heroes—in which the heroes embody the virtues necessary for social life beyond that of the first families, led by the first fathers, who have come to form marriages as the result of their experience of Jove—their fear of Jove leads them to a second passion, that of shame or modesty (*pudore*), that causes them to control their bodies and passions. The power of imaginative universals is extended to form the meaning of the heroes. Thus Achilles is the imaginative universal of bravery or courage and all individuals who are brave are literally Achilles. They are not *like* Achilles or analogous to Achilles; rather, Achilles is equally them and himself. In giving another example, Vico says: "Just so the Egyptians reduced to the genus 'civil sage' all their inventions useful or necessary to the human race which are particular effects of civil wisdom, and because they could not abstract the intelligible genus 'civil sage,' much less the form of civil wisdom in which these Egyptians were sages, they imaged it forth as Thrice-great Hermes" (209).

Through imagination or *fantasia* a particular can be universally predicated of any number of particulars, just as the property of bravery or courage can be rationally predicated of a group of individuals. But this rational or logical relationship based on the abstract universal presupposes the imaginative universal. Philosophical wisdom is not possible except as a development of poetic wisdom. Achilles or Thrice-great Hermes comes first. They must be imagined, made as poetic characters, before they can be thought, that is, made intelligible as particular instances of class concepts. When they can be so thought the mind has passed into the age of humans—Vico's third age—the age in which custom gives way to written law and reflection arises as the means to assert truths of experience.

In this third age, *fantasia* is not lost. It takes the form of the aesthetic, not the mythic or the Vichian poetic wisdom. Cassirer, in *Language and*

Myth, develops the point: "If language is to grow into a vehicle of thought, an expression of concepts and judgments, this evolution can be achieved only at the price of foregoing the wealth and fullness of immediate experience. In the end, what is left of the concrete sense and feeling content it once possessed is little more than a bare skeleton." This original power to capture in language the immediate is now possible only through artistic expression. "Here," Cassirer says, "it recovers the fullness of life; but it is no longer a life mythically bound and fettered, but an esthetically liberated life. . . . What poetry expresses is neither the mythic word-picture of gods and daemons, nor the logical truth of abstract determinations and relations. The world of poetry stands apart from both, as a world of illusion and fantasy."

But this world of poetry is not illusion and fantasy in the sense of something unreal or irrational, that is, something without true meaning or sense. The mind still capable of the power of the metaphor in Vico's third age is liberated to act according to its own principles. As Cassirer concludes: "This liberation is achieved not because the mind throws aside the sensuous forms of word and image, but in that it uses them both as organs of its own, and thereby recognizes them for what they really are: forms of its own self-revelation."[16]

Poetry is our only means to recollect that original sense of the world and word out of which the human world has been made. Imagination, then, is memory. When the poetic imagination brings these *archai* forth they are the self in an interior monologue with itself. Is it possible for us to achieve a language of imaginative universals that we can encounter in aesthetic terms? For the world of myth, like the world of the child, is in itself closed to us. The world itself is already formed. It cannot be remade except in the dream to which we have access and which has a logic that is one with mythic thought. We come into this world of the dream only at night. In the dream all the gods and demons come forth. They become available.

Joyce's poetic problem, seen in this way, is to ask whether there is a way to move words against themselves so that they will actually reveal what Vico calls the common mental dictionary (*dizionario mentale comune*), that is, the very sense-making power of the imagination that lies behind every language and which every language is trying to express in its own grammar and vocabulary (162, 445). To do this, *verba* must be taken back to *res* via etymology. It completes the project begun in Plato's *Cratylus*.

But this requires not an ordinary etymology of the history of words moving back into their past in the manner of a lexicon. It requires an etymology of coincidence in which words overlap with each other and with their own meanings such that they are continually meeting each other and taking us, as readers, along with them until senses of the self and world are generated that could not in principle be anticipated. Like Gödel's incompleteness theorem in mathematical logic, in Joyce's linguistic coincidences we are never at a point where we can assert, "That's all." In *Finnegans Wake* we come as close as we can, short of a regression to the mythic mind as such, to thinking in terms of imaginative universals.

Joyce's Jokes

Joyce's apology, that Plato calls for, from the poets, in his quarrel with the poets, is in the geometry lesson in the classbook section of the *Wake*. He does this through Plato's name: "P.t.l.o.a.t.o."—"Please to lick one and turn over" (286.03), which he repeats as "plates to lick one and turn over" ("plates" is a pun on a possible way to pronounce "please"; *plato* [Spanish] = plate) (286.18). Take a lick (a look) at Plato and turn over. Take a lick from Plato's quarrel and turn over. Joyce inverts the terms of the quarrel so that poetry takes charge of philosophy. Just as Joyce said, he did not attempt to square the circle but instead circled the square.[17] No one was allowed to enter the Platonic Academy who did not know mathematics. Joyce's poetry disrupts the quarrel ("of an hour") with its puns, its madness, its *folie*—"philophosy," "phullupsuppy of a plate o'monkynous." Philosophy should not take itself so seriously, for its love of wisdom is also a kind of madness, a rational madness.

Aristotle says that *anthropos* is the only animal that laughs.[18] Laughter that has a point is always ironic. The modern poet, freed from the confines of myth, not only employs metaphor, as does the philosopher, but can employ the philosopher's trope of irony. Socrates does not own irony. The poet not of the Homeric age but of the third age of ideal eternal history has the power of irony and through it has access to the distinctive power of the self as human. Joyce described *Work in Progress* to the Danish writer Tom Kristensen as above all a work of humor. Joyce said: "Now they're bombing Spain. Isn't it better to make a great joke instead, as I have done?"[19]

Joyce is quite serious that *Finnegans Wake* is best described as a great joke. It is a comedy. Joyce's "nightmaze" (411.08) does not include the nightmares of history—what Hegel would call the labor of the negative (*Arbeit des Negativen*). If history is itself a nightmare, in Joyce's dream we escape from it or at least receive relief from it. Beckett's observation is correct that in regard to the *Divine Comedy* the *Wake* corresponds to

Purgatorio, because in Purgatory there is a continual process of opposites at work, such as Vice and Virtue. The Inferno is not in it, nor is Paradiso, because Joyce's "providentiality" is the fourth age of the cycles of history, not a divine order beyond history (on this point Joyce differs from Vico). *Finnegans Wake* can be called simply a comedy—the title by which Dante himself called his poem. The "Divine" was added later.

If we approach *Finnegans Wake* as a joke book, it humanizes us. We stop taking ourselves seriously and see that every word is a pun, a coincidence with its own multiple meanings and with those other words we are encouraged to associate with it. Out of Plato's cave we are on top of the world, able to see what we will without concern for reason or for purpose, for as we have been told at the outset, we are in a "commodious vicus of recirculation." Our memory is jogged. To think along with what we are reading we must begin continually to remember anything and all that we have ever learned, thought, or read elsewhere. The three functions of Vico's memory are at work: memory (*memoria*) when it remembers things, imagination (*fantasia*) when it alters or simulates them, and ingenuity (*ingegno*) when it puts them into a new relationship or gives them a new turn (819). But we are remembering to no particular purpose, just recalling things for the sake of recalling them and enjoying the act of recall. It is not Plato's *anamnēsis*, it is the "storiella as she is syung" (267.07–8). Our recollection is musical, just as Vico says language was originally sung, when it was young.

Terence White Gervais, a visitor to Joyce in the late 1930s, asked him if his book was a blending of literature and music. Joyce replied, "No, it's pure music." Then, on being asked if it contained levels of meaning, Joyce replied, "No, no, it's meant to make you laugh." He told Jacques Mercanton: "I am only an Irish clown, a great joker at the universe." To a drinking companion, he once corrected *In vino veritas* to *In risu veritas*. In replying to why he had written the book the way he did, he said: "To keep the critics busy for three hundred years."[20] He signed a letter to Harriet Shaw Weaver (November 15, 1926) containing a key to a draft of the first lines of *Finnegans Wake*: "Jeems Jokes."[21]

It is unlikely that Joyce's apology as a response to the quarrel of an hour would gain him admission to Plato's city in speech. He likely will need to find a place in the garden outside the city walls or to find another city where philosophers do not rule. In the *Laws* Plato says that the state put forth in the *Republic* described a city for only the gods or the children of gods.[22] It is the ideal polis that can be projected from the best the Athenians have to offer. In this nearly divine city there is no place reserved for a maker of jokes, even though the idea of a philosopher-king is quite likely intended by Socrates as an ironic suggestion, a requirement that can never be fulfilled in order to make the city in speech become actual.

What are we to think of Joyce's claim that *Finnegans Wake* is a great joke? Is it serious humor that is also an instruction for us not to take ourselves seriously? Is Joyce's claim of a joke itself intended as a joke? "Joke" is most immediately from Latin *jocus*, "jest," "joke," "game," and is akin to Old Saxon and Old High German *gehan*, "to say," "speak," and related to Middle Welsh *leith*, "language," that can be taken back to Sanskrit *yācati*, "he implores," with the basic meaning of speaking. To joke is to speak, spoke. Joke is associated in the *Wake* with Finnegan: "Mark Time's Finist Joke"—Mark Tim Finnegan's Joke; Time's Final (Finest) Joke, i.e., death (455.29). Also, "What boyazhness! Sole shadow shows. Tis jest jibberweek's joke" (565.13–14) (boojazn, Russian "fear"); recalls the song "Finnegan's Wake"; "like blazes," Jabberwocky's joke, jest. Fear of the Shadow (of death), a joke. Also, "Jests, jokes, jigs and jorums for the Wake lent from the properties of the late cemented Mr. T. M. Finnegan" (221.26–27).

The Ballad of Tim Finnegan is a joke, a jest. Doused with whiskey, "Timothy rising from the bed, says, 'whirl your liquor round like blazes, Thanam o'n dhoul, do ye think I'm dead." Finnegan wakes at his own wake and speaks. A joke is a joy. Joyce makes jokes a way of speaking. Every line in the *Wake* is a joke, a juxtaposition of one meaning on another; no word is allowed to stand alone, to have a literal meaning; every word coincides with another.

The title, *Finnegans Wake*, is itself an imaginative universal that is also a joke: *fine* Italian "end" with the *n* doubled, again. It is the name of one person and also all such persons, since it is a plural, not a possessive. Unlike Achilles, however, it does not embody a virtue. Finnegan is not heroic, he is comic as he is resurrected by the whiskey spilled on his body. Instead it is a juxtaposition—the end again. In the beginning is the end; just as the text itself begins. A wake is of course also a beginning and an end.

Joyce can be at home in Vico's Augustinian "great city of the human race," for there are no restrictions on imagination in the *New Science*. Vico's magnet is the opposite of Occam's razor: all in the human world is drawn into Vico's science, into his great ideal city in speech. It is ideal because Vico's "eternal history" is "ideal eternal history." The particular customs, laws, deeds, and languages of the nations at war and in peace that are the subject of philology are joined with philosophy, that undertakes to examine them as they can be made to fit into its universal order of the *corso* and *ricorso* of gods, heroes, and humans. Like Joyce, Vico excludes nothing in the *New Science*—as in the *Wake*, "here comes everybody." The *New Science*, like *Finnegans Wake*, is intended as a complete speech, a theater of the world in which all of human memory abounds and makes its appearance.

Vico's book is a book of wisdom, generated from poetic wisdom, one in which poetry is necessary for philosophy and in which the poet can feel at home. It is built upon an irony captured in Vico's claim that the true is the made and thus convertible with the made—*verum esse ipsum factum* and *verum et factum convertuntur*. Just at the point when the modern science of nature is transforming "natural philosophy" into science itself, taking the name of science for itself, its own identity, Vico makes a distinction between *scientia* as the form of thinking in which the object of thought is made by the thinker, as in mathematics and history, such that the thinker can have a complete knowledge of the object, and *conscientia* or consciousness, which can witness or recognize its object but does not make it.[23] Vico steals the term "science" and declares modern science to be only a form of consciousness. It is a theft completed by Hegel when he declares his *Phenomenology of Spirit* to be "the science [*Wissenschaft*] of the experience of consciousness." The only real science is philosophical science, a science of the whole, which is human wisdom itself.

Natural science is *conscientia*, not *scientia*, because the objects it knows are of a different order of being than that of the thinker. The objects of nature are made by God alone, who makes by knowing and knows by making. Thus we can only have a true science of history because man makes it. The science of nature is an elaborate witnessing of natural objects and events, based on experiment, because in experiment we simulate making but cannot actually make what we come to recognize through it. Just as the sciences of nature are becoming science, Vico deprives them of the term. Vico's philosophy of history is a wake in which the nations in their *corso* and *ricorso* seem to be dead, and rise again—all at the direction of providence that rules the great city in which they cycle. Vico makes in speech this life of nations which is originally made in the movements of history.

Joyce's city in speech is Dublin. Joyce once said of Dublin: "You see I carry this city around with me always."[24] Joyce introduces Dublin to us in a joke on the first page of the *Wake*, where he speaks of "topsawyer's rocks by the stream Oconee exaggerated themselse to Laurens County's gorgios while they went doublin their mumper all the time" (03.07–9). His reference is to Dublin, Georgia, connecting the new world with the old. In his letter to Harriet Shaw Weaver supplying her with a key to this page, Joyce says the motto of Dublin, Georgia, founded by a Dubliner named Sawyer and located on the Oconee River, is "doublin all the time."[25] Whether this actually is the town's motto or whether Joyce created it is not known to me. I think he made it up. Julien Levy found three Dublins in the United States when Joyce asked him to discover if there were any Dublins in America.[26] In Georgia, Dublin lies between Atlanta ("the choicest and the cheapest from Atlanta to Oconee, while I'll be drowsing in the garden") (140.35–36) and Savannah. Joyce would be glad to know that Dublin has doubled, as there is today, across the Oconee, an East Dublin. Thus the gorgios, as Joyce predicted, have doubled their mumper, their number.

Dublin is a city in speech because it is continually created by Joyce, who has left its physical environs but, as he said, it is always with him, from *Dubliners* to *Finnegans Wake*. More than anything else, more than all the specific references one can find to it, Dublin is behind the principle of doubleness that dominates Joyce's imagination. All is double, from Shem the penman and Shaun the postman, throughout the *Wake*. It is the coincidence of opposites that Joyce finds in the philosophy of Bruno the Nolan. Vico is Joyce's double because the double of Shem is Shaun, Giovanni, John the post around which Joyce writes the *Wake*. He is "Old Vico Roundpoint" (260.14–15). He is Joyce's "roundhead staple of other days to rise in undress maisonry upstanded (joygrantit!)" (4.34–35).

Vico, in the *New Science*, proceeds on the basis that if Rome can be understood in terms of his principles of history then all nations can be understood in a similar fashion. In like manner, we may say if Joyce could understand Dublin, then he could understand all of the human condition. Dublin is the microcosm of the human, the guide to entering into it at all points. It was the luck of the Irish for Joyce to be born there. And it is the wit of the Irish on which Joyce could rely to take him through the "nightmaze" (411.08) of the *Wake*.

As the French critic Louis Gillet wrote: "Of course, it is no longer a question of Time and Space in this indivisible duration where the absolute reigns. These two comrades, who did their cooking for so long on the scrap-iron stove of Kantian categories, find their pot knocked over by a kick from James Joyce. Their soup is spilled out—chronology disappears and all the centuries are contemporary."[27] We turn over any page, round any corner in Joyce's city, and we encounter again the visitor from Neapolis, with his companion the Nolan, just as we do on the first page, as we go "past Eve and Adam's"—and they have everything we need to assure our attendance at the *Wake*.

Chapter 1

✦

Beckett's Exagmination

Recommended Reading

In a letter to Harriet Shaw Weaver on May 21, 1926, Joyce wrote: "There is a book on Bruno (though not on Nolan) by Lewis McIntyre (Macmillan). I do not know if Vico has been translated. I would not pay overmuch attention to these theories, beyond using them for all they are worth, but they have gradually forced themselves on me through circumstances of my own life."[1]

Adaline Glasheen, in the entry for Vico in the *Third Census of "Finnegans Wake,"* remarks on this letter that "unfortunately, knowledge of this work [*New Science*] has not forced itself on Joyceans, who by and large read it in an abridgement which omits much that matters in FW; and I find it generally supposed that *The New Science* is little more than an almost invisible scaffolding which encloses FW and is unnecessary to an understanding of FW." She then concludes: "I don't agree, and direct the reader (for starters) to Samuel Beckett's essay in *Our Exagmination*."[2] The abridged edition to which Glasheen refers reduces Vico's text by about one-third.[3] Joyce, of course, read the work in its full text and in the original.

Joyce may have come to know of Vico in the courses and conversations he had as a student of the Jesuit Father Charles Ghezzi, lecturer in Italian at University College, Dublin. He had ongoing discussions with Ghezzi on Italian literature and philosophy.[4] Joyce learned Italian, acquired a good grounding in Dante, and discovered Bruno in his university years. In the standard Catholic interpretation of Vico's thought, in the late nineteenth century, Vico was regarded as the only truly Catholic Italian philosopher who could be pitted against the philosophers of modern Europe, whose ideas mostly had roots in the Reformation.[5] Joyce's school friend Constantine Curran reports that one of the assigned readings of Joyce's college course in 1901 was Raffaello Fornaciari's *Disegno storico della letteratura italiana* (*Historical Outline of Italian Literature*): "The references to Bruno and to Vico, to the intuitional and pantheistic mode of Bruno's thinking; to the indeterminate, encyclopedic sweep of mind which makes Vico, as Fornaciari says, an inexhaustible mine for future quarrying are sufficient to set an intelligence less alert than Joyce's upon inquiry."[6]

In 1901, in his pamphlet on the Irish theater, "The Day of the Rabblement," Joyce began with a reference to Bruno as "the Nolan." The following year, in the conclusion to his essay on the poet James Clarence Mangan, Joyce wrote of being enclosed in history, of legend moving down "the cycles," such that "the ancient gods, who are visions of the divine names, die and come to life many times," and that "in those vast courses which enfold us and in that great memory which is greater and more generous than our memory, no life, no moment of exaltation is ever lost."[7] It is uncertain what Joyce's source may be for these views, but they are sufficiently Vichian that they could come directly from the *New Science*, in which all of history is a great memory theater, all of the events in which are repetitions.

Several years later Joyce arrived in Trieste, and began giving English lessons at the Berlitz School. He resided in via Donato Bramante at the Piazza Giambattista Vico, an address he chose deliberately.[8] From 1911 to 1913 Joyce gave English lessons to Paolo Cuzzi, as mentioned earlier, who later became an eminent Triestine lawyer. Cuzzi was then studying Vico in school and he discovered that Joyce had a passionate interest in Vico.[9] In 1911 Croce's *La filosofia di Giambattista Vico* appeared, and in this same year appeared the first two volumes (vols. 4 and 5) of the modern Laterza edition of Vico's *Opere*, under the editorship of Croce and Fausto Nicolini: *La scienza nuova seconda* and *L'Autobiografia*.

Joyce was reminded of Vico every day, when crossing Piazza Giambattista Vico, or circling the square; he was also in the middle of a Vichian renaissance. He knew Croce's earlier *Estetica* (1902), a copy of which he had borrowed from his friend in Trieste, Dario de Tuoni, and which contains an important chapter on Vico.[10] In 1914, the year Joyce finished *A Portrait*, volume 1 of the Laterza edition appeared, containing Vico's *De antiquissima Italorum sapientia* (*On the Most Ancient Wisdom of the Italians*) that is worked into the Latin passage quoted on Bruno and Vico in *Finnegans Wake*. If Joyce read Vico or some of Vico earlier it might have been in one of the volumes of the nineteenth-century Ferrari edition, *Opere di Giambattista Vico* (2nd ed., 1852–54) or in the Pomodoro edition that imitated it (1858–69), or in any one of the numerous nineteenth-century single-volume reprintings of the *Scienza nuova*.

In the Cornell collection of Joyce's papers are three pages of typescript that are a copy of the last three paragraphs of the Vico entry for the eleventh edition of the *Encyclopaedia Britannica* (1910–11), followed by passages in Italian, the source for which is probably Croce's *La filosofia di Giambattista Vico*. The typescript was likely done near the time of the appearance of these works, during Joyce's Trieste period. The pages show that Joyce was collecting material on Vico's *Scienza nuova*; they do not express original views of Joyce on Vico.[11]

Joyce knew Jules Michelet's French edition of *La scienza nuova* and Vico's autobiography, which included a translation of the *De antiquissima* and extracts from other of Vico's works (1835). Joyce also would have known Vico's *De nostri temporis studiorum ratione* from its publication in the first volume of the Laterza edition and from extracts from it included in the Michelet translation. In his French studies at university Joyce read Michelet in 1901. Michelet had been encouraged by Victor Cousin to translate Vico. Cousin, who lectured in 1828 at the Sorbonne on the philosophy of history, including Vico's, had also encouraged Edgar Quinet to translate Herder. Herder's and Vico's ideas form the basis of Quinet's *Introduction à la philosophie de l'histoire de l'humanité*. Joyce quotes a passage regarding cycles of history of Quinet's work almost verbatim in French in *Finnegans Wake*, concerning how in history "the cities have changed masters and names" (281.04–13).

This passage is parodied four times at full or nearly full length: it is made Irish (14.35–15.11); is made to play on Romulus and Remus (236.19–32); is associated with the image of the world as originally a garden (354.22–36); and is part of his paragraph on the "vicociclometer" (615.02–9).[12] Joyce had committed this passage from Quinet's work to memory and once quoted it to John Sullivan, the Irish tenor, as they walked by the cemetery in Paris on the Boulevard Edgar Quinet.[13] Joyce combines Bruno and Vico with the two French philosophers of history: "The olold stoliolum! From quiqui quinet to michemiche chelet and a jambebatiste to a brulobrulo!" (117.10–12).

Joyce recommended Michelet's translation to friends who wished to understand Vico but did not read Italian. In talking with Joyce in 1927 about *Work in Progress*, Padraic Colum reports: "Joyce suggested I should read Vico. But had Vico been translated into a language I could read? Yes, Michelet had translated him into French."[14] Instead Colum read the article on Vico in the *Encyclopaedia Britannica*. When Constantine Curran visited Joyce in 1921, Joyce introduced him to Vico's *Scienza nuova*, pointing out its importance for his *Work in Progress*. Joyce took Michelet's translation from his shelf and lent it to Curran, directing his attention to a passage in Michelet's introduction which says that Vico's thought is obscure and bizarre but that in a system presented in this manner there is "une grandeur imposante et une sombre poésie qui fait penser à celle de Dante."[15] In a letter of May 13, 1927, to Harriet Shaw Weaver, Joyce explained his idea of the Phoenix as a "symbol used by Michelet to explain Vico's theory."[16]

Joyce urged Weaver to read Vico to understand his new project of *Work in Progress*, as he had urged her to read the *Odyssey* to understand *Ulysses*.[17] In the key he sent her to the draft of the first page of his work, he wrote: "passencore = pas encore and *ricorsi storici* of Vico."[18] In October 1923 he sent her some early pages of the *Wake*, remarking: "Perhaps the theory of history so well set forth (after Hegel and Giambattista Vico) by the four eminent annalists who are even now treading the typepress in sorrow will explain part of my meaning."[19]

Vico and Hegel are the two founders of the modern philosophy of history. Although Hegel has a method of dialectic in which *Geist* develops by turning back upon itself (his doctrine of *Aufhebung*) and he regards his whole system and the system of the whole to be a circle of circles, he does not have a conception of *ricorsi storici*. Hegel never mentions Vico and may never have known of him. His philosophy of history is in no sense influenced by Vico. Joyce may mention Vico and Hegel together because of his awareness of Croce's interpretation of Vico, in which Croce makes Vico into the Italian Hegel, bypassing much of what Joyce finds in Vico, namely, the radical significance of the imaginative universal and the origination of consciousness in poetic wisdom or myth, which is not to be found in Hegel.[20] Croce's desire for a historical connection of Hegel to Vico led him to write his fictional account of Hegel being introduced to Vico's thought late in life and declaring that Vico's views were close to his own.[21]

Padraic Colum reports that, on one of his walks with Joyce in Paris: "'Of course,' Joyce told me, 'I don't take Vico's speculations literally; I use his cycles as a trellis.'"[22] This comment is well known and is likely much of the basis for many interpreters having claimed that Vico's work functions simply as the "invisible scaffolding" to which Glasheen refers. Joyce's remark to Colum appears casual, but in fact it is clever and precise. A trellis is a structure of latticework for the support of climbing plants. It is also possible to speak of "a trellis of interlacing streams." Etymologically "trellis" is a fabric of coarse weave and specifically *trilicius* (Vulgar Latin) is "woven with triple thread." "Trellis" has within it the notion of three (*tres*). A trellis as a scaffolding is the least of these meanings, as it is static. In the *Wake* all the streams interlace and in the fabric of the *Wake* all is woven together in crisscross, as Joyce reformulates Vico's three ages and three principles of humanity to include a fourth—providence.

Joyce restudied Vico to write *Finnegans Wake*. In March 1925, while suffering with his failing eyesight, he wrote to Weaver: "I should like to hear Vico read to me again in the hope that someday I may be able to write again. I put an advertisement in the Mail for a reader but got not even one reply though I have often seen advertisements from Italians in it."[23] In 1940 he wrote Jacques Mercanton asking him to get a copy of a book on Vico of which he had heard.[24] It was H. P. Adams's *Life and Writings of Giambattista Vico* (1935), the only study written on Vico in English since the early and very good study by Robert Flint, *Vico*, written for Blackwood's series of "Philosophical Classics for English Readers" in 1884, a work which Joyce likely knew: "A chip off the old Flint" (83.10).[25] In discussing *Work in Progress* with Joyce, Mercanton brought up Michelet's *Vico*. Joyce told him: "I don't know whether Vico's theory is true; it doesn't matter. It's useful to me; that's what counts."[26]

After the publication of *Finnegans Wake* Joyce wrote to Mercanton about its reception. There had been only a few, odd reviews; Joyce quoted from one in a Roman journal: "'Seeing that the whole book is founded on the work of an Italian thinker' . . . ?" Joyce included the ellipses and question mark as a literary shrug of his shoulders, as though to say: Is it not obvious that the book is founded on Vico? He said the response to *Finnegans Wake* was "a complete fiasco up to the present as far as European criticism is concerned."[27]

Heinrich Straumann, professor of English literature at the University of Zurich, contacted Joyce in the winter of 1941, requesting to meet with him. Joyce agreed; their conversation took place at dinner in a restaurant on the Bellvueplatz. He reported that Joyce had "an expression of friendly irony" and "led the conversation with a certain light objectivity, as one who has a perfectly well defined attitude towards most things but who is quite ready to revise his thinking with regard to their relationship to each other; almost more like a philosopher than an artist." Straumann says: "We conversed in the German language, which he seemed to speak with absolute facility, and he was seldom at a loss for a word."

Straumann asked if a knowledge of local conditions in Dublin would give him better access to the comprehension of *Finnegans Wake*, and Joyce "replied firmly in the negative. One should not pay any particular attention to the allusions to place-names, historical events, literary happenings and personalities, but let the literary phenomenon affect one as such. If a premise to the reading of the work must be sought, then it should be a knowledge of the philosopher Giambattista Vico, to whom he was greatly indebted. It was evident that Joyce was particularly attracted by the encyclopedic features of Vico's system. But Vico's insistence upon the social element of all cultural achievements as well as his apperception of a linguistic basis as its premise seemed also to have made a very strong impression."[28] A few days later Straumann learned that Joyce was seriously ill, and then came the news of his death. Straumann spoke at Joyce's funeral, as representative of the university.

Joyce's recommendation of how to read *Finnegans Wake* was twofold—to read it and let what was said affect one as such, and if a premise to the reading was sought, the reader should turn to the philosopher Vico. The importance of Vico for understanding his work was Joyce's earliest and his last recommendation, as well as the recommendation that he consistently gave throughout the years of its writing. Joyce took on the whole of Vico—his conception of time, of memory and imagination, of myth, of etymology, of providence, of the principles of humanity. And Joyce, as will be shown, took on the figure of Vico himself, who, as Vico says in his autobiography, fell and rose up again, and, after publishing his major work, the *Scienza nuova*, lived in his own city as a stranger, an expatriate in his own *patria*.

Beckett's Reading

Samuel Beckett read *Work in Progress* and Croce's *La filosofia di Giambattista Vico*, as well as *La scienza nuova*, the *Divina Commedia*, and other of Dante's major works. He knew the doctrine of opposites of Bruno, perhaps taking it from the concluding dialogue of Bruno's *De la causa principio et uno*. These all appear in Beckett's "Dante . . . Bruno. Vico . . Joyce," the lead essay in *Our Exagmination Round His Factification for Incamination of Work in Progress* (1929).[29] Beckett was introduced to Joyce when he arrived in Paris in November 1928. In December, Joyce suggested he write the essay—and the topic to write it on—for *Our Exagmination*. In June the essay appeared in *transition*, at Joyce's urging, set from the proofs of the volume. Beckett had just turned twenty-three. It was his first published essay.

H. S. Harris, the Hegelian philosopher and scholar of the Italian Idealism of Croce and Gentile, echoes Glasheen's judgment on the importance of Beckett's essay and of the general failure of Joyce interpretation since its publication to pursue in any depth the connection of Vico and Joyce. He points out that Joyce's comment to Colum concerning using Vico's cycles as a trellis had the effect, instead of stirring interest in Vico as a basis for

Joyce's work, of making Joyce scholars think that all that was needed in this regard was to assert that Vico provided a framework or scaffold on which to place his ideas. An example is the approach of Anthony Burgess. Although Burgess rightly identifies the *New Science* as the book Joyce employed as a backbone of *Finnegans Wake*, as mentioned earlier, he claims that "the backbone of *Finnegans Wake* is easily filleted out."[30] Indeed, it is filleted out quite simply, by Burgess, in a single paragraph characterizing Vico's three ages of history. Apparently he thinks nothing more is required to understand Vico's connection to Joyce. Harris says: "Nothing that I have seen in my own tongue (except that first article of Beckett's) is worth the paper it is printed on as an interpretation of what Vico meant to Joyce."[31] Harris, like Glasheen, points us back to Beckett.

Joyce says, of the authors of the twelve essays in the volume: "I did stand behind those twelve Marshals more or less directing them what lines of research to follow."[32] The title is from a line in Joyce's work (497.02). "Exagmination" is "examination" merged with Latin *agmen* (a mass of persons in movement, an army on the march, a stream). "Incamination" contains a play on the Italian verb *incamminare*—"to put on the right road" (the Vico road, that "goes round and round")—and on *factum* ("what is made," Vico's principle of *verum esse ipsum factum*, "the true is the made").

If we consider the whole passage as it appears in *Finnegans Wake*, the title is part of a Vichian statement: "If there is a future in every past that is present *Quis est qui non novit quinnigan* and *Qui quae quot at Quinnigan's Quake*! Stump! His producers are they not his consumers? Your exagmination round his factification for incamination of a warping process. Declaim!" (496.35–36–497.03). Who is there who did not know Finnegan? How many? The answer is everybody is at Finnegan's wake. "Quinnigan's Quake" is the quake of fear felt by the *giganti* or Vico's protohumans, who respond to the thunderous sky by naming it "Jove" and thus beginning gentile history.

The producers of this history of the nations are also the consumers of it. Since human beings have made history out of their own natures, they can make a knowledge of it. Thus they consume what they themselves have made. It is a warping process, in which what is made is bent back upon itself, a process of self-knowledge. It all originates from the giants' power to Declaim!—to speak out the thunder as the first name, Jove—from which all language, as well as culture, begins. The passage from which *Our Exagmination* takes its title is fully Vichian.

The title of Beckett's essay leaves no doubt as to how the reader is to approach *Work in Progress*. It is a tetralogy, with Joyce as one of its four terms: "Dante . . . Bruno. Vico . . Joyce"—with no dot or period after Joyce. Beckett discusses each of these figures but gives no explanation in the essay of the structure of the title or its significance. I have three thoughts on it; one is chronological, another is linguistic, and the third is textual. Chronologically, between the birthdates of Dante (1265) and Bruno (1548), approximately three centuries intervene; between Bruno and Vico (1668), one century; and between Vico and Joyce (1882), two centuries. The reader of *Work in Progress* is reminded of the sequence of these figures in history, with Joyce now taking his place in line. The dates of the two literary figures who run throughout the work, Shakespeare and Swift, correspond closely with those of Bruno and Vico, and if they were substituted for Bruno and Vico, they would provide a literary sequence from Dante to Joyce.

Linguistically, the title contains two sentences. The first has an ellipsis between Dante and Bruno. Omitted is how we are to comprehend the movement from Dante the poet-in-exile to Bruno the philosopher-heretic who, as Joyce says through Stephen Dedalus, "was terribly burned."[33] The second sentence is incomplete because what Joyce is and how we are to understand him is not yet finished. The ellipsis between Vico and Joyce is only partial because the gap between Vico the exile in his own *patria*, and Joyce the expatriate, is not great. Vico is recycled in Joyce. The first "sentence" and the second can be juxtaposed or "recoursed." Vico carefully asserts that his views are for the greater glory of the Christian religion, but his cyclic concept of history is wholly pagan, presided over by a providence that does not lead to a final day of resurrection. Joyce is not a heretic but a permanently lapsed Catholic whose world in *Work in Progress*, as Beckett explains, corresponds to Purgatory.

A further and broad textual Vichian reading of the title is that the four figures suggest Joyce's transposition of Vico's three ages into his four ages. Dante, as Vico calls him, is the "Tuscan Homer." He is the transmitter of the divine age of the *ricorso*. Bruno, burned at the stake for his views, is the hero and even the author of a work on heroes, *Gli eroici furori*—"to the heroicised furibouts of the Nolanus theory" (163.23–24). Vico is the scientist of history. Joyce is the agent of the providential order which connects all things as "cocoincidences."

The number four, for Joyce, as well as three times four, or twelve, is fundamental. In a conversation with Adolph Hoffmeister in 1930, Joyce said: "Number is an enigma that God deciphers. Along with Beckett, a small, red-haired Irishman and my great friend, I have discovered the importance of numbers in life and history. Dante was obsessed by the number three. He divided his poem into three parts, each with thirty-three cantos, written in terza rima. And why always the arrangement of four—four legs of a table, four legs of a horse, four seasons of the year, four provinces of Ireland? Why are there twelve tables of the law, twelve Apostles, twelve months, and twelve Napoleon's marshals?"[34] He made a similar comment to Padraic Colum regarding the four Evangelists and the four Masters who compiled the annals of Ireland: "'Twelve is the public number' he said, 'twelve hours of the day, twelve men on a jury.'"[35]

Beckett's essay, the first of the twelve in the volume, in its fourfold title has a resonance with the "'Mamma Lujah' known to every schoolboy scandaller, be he Matty, Marky, Lukey or John-a-Donk" (614.28–30) of the "millwheeling vicociclometer." The first three figures of Beckett's title are like the first three Evangelists or authors of the "synoptic" Gospels (from Greek *synoptikos*, "view together"). Dante, Bruno, and Vico comprise a whole. But the fourth Gospel, John, presents a puzzle because it relates all of the details of Jesus's ministry differently. Joyce's work is a unique variant on the combined account of the three Italians, retelling what they have told in a new way. Joyce recourses their *corso*.

Beckett begins by calling attention to how Vico has folded philosophy and philology into each other as a single method. In the *New Science*, Vico says "philosophy undertakes to examine philology" (7). Philosophy fails by half in directing its efforts toward the true (*il vero*) as the universal in human nature, and philology fails by half in directing its efforts toward the certain (*il certo*) that is composed of those particular acts, done by human choice.

Beckett opposes Croce's view of Vico: "It pleases Croce to consider him as a mystic, essentially speculative, '*disdegnoso dell'empirismo*.'"[36] Croce's *La filosofia di Giambattista Vico* (1911) was the standard comprehensive interpretation of Vico's philosophy of the day.[37] The sentence in full that Beckett quotes is "Ora, l'ispirazione del Vico era genuinamente ed esclusivamente teoretica, punto pratica o riformistica; altamente speculativo il suo metodo a disdegnoso dell'empirismo; idealistico, e perciò antimaterialistico e antiutilitaristico, il suo spirito." ("Now, Vico's inspiration was genuinely and exclusively theoretical, not at all practical or reformulatory, his method was deeply speculative and distaining of empiricism; his spirit was idealistic and thus antimaterialistic and antiutilitarian").[38]

For Croce to claim Vico is "deeply speculative" is not the same as to claim that he is a mystic. Croce was a Hegelian and thus by "speculative" he is likely referring to Hegel's sense of speculation as captured in the "*spekulativer Satz*" or "speculative sentence," upon which Hegel claims his manner of thinking is based, and he likely has in mind Hegel's overriding contrast between speculation that is the thought of reason (*Vernunft*) and thought based on reflection or understanding (*Verstand*).[39] By saying that Vico disdained empiricism, Croce means that Vico's method rejects the philosophical doctrine that all thought derives from sense impressions, as is to be found in Locke and British Empiricism generally. In claiming this, Croce is not claiming that Vico disdains the empirical in human existence. For Croce, Vico was the Italian Hegel, having a philosophy of objective idealism based on forming the results of all the particular sciences into a comprehensive system.

Where Beckett's understanding of Vico really divides from Croce's is in Beckett's grasp of the fundamental importance of Vico's conception of poetic characters or imaginative universals (*caratteri poetici o universali fantastici*). Beckett loosely cites Vico's line in the *New Science* declaring that the discovery of this original form of language is *la chiave maestra* or "master key" to his science that cost him a good twenty years to accomplish (34). As Vico says: "the first science to be learned should be mythology or interpretation of fables" (51).

Beckett characterizes Vico as "a practical roundheaded Neapolitan." This is a statement taken directly from Joyce. In *A Portrait* Stephen refers to his Italian teacher Father Ghezzi as "little roundhead rogue'seye Ghezzi."[40] Padraic Colum, the Irish poet and playwright, reported that on one of their walks in Paris in about 1927, discussing *Work in Progress*, Joyce referred to Vico in a similar fashion: "'He was one of those round-headed Neapolitan men,' Joyce told me. I forget whom he mentioned as another of them."[41]

The other was quite likely Bruno of Nola, since Nola is part of the commune of Naples. In the *Wake*, at the beginning of the classbook section, in which all of Vico's terminology is glossed in its marginalia, is "Old Vico Roundpoint" (260.15–16). "Roundhead" is not a term known to me, nor to the *Oxford English Dictionary*, except in its Cromwellian associations, which do not seem to fit, given Cromwell's treatment of the Irish. The Vico road goes round and round, but to derive "roundheaded" from this seems trite or at least not especially clever, not representative of Joyce's linguistic complexity. In Beckett's context of criticizing what he takes to be Croce's view of Vico, the term seems to mean "hardheaded," empirically minded, thinking in relation to facts, and probably a bit stubborn. In a novel about academic life, *Matricide at St. Martha's* (1995), by the Dublin-born Ruth Dudley Edwards, appears the comment: "'You need the whistle-blowers and the people who don't mind being unpopular and the people with tunnel vision.' 'But not too many of them,' said the Bursar. 'They're almost all Roundheads.'"[42]

The term Beckett settles on, for Vico, is "Vico, the scientific historian."[43] A case can be made for this as a precise designation for Vico.

Broadly speaking, Vico can be called a philosopher or a philosopher of history, but he is most correctly an advocate of his own "new science," which is made up of both philosophical reasoning and philological analysis. Beckett rightly insists that Vico's unique conception of providence is fundamental to this science. Vico uses *provvedenza*, *provvidenza* in 120 lines in the *New Science*, spread throughout the text of the work.[44] Vico is a "new scientist" whose science is governed by providence, making it a form of divine science.

The definition Beckett quotes in Italian is quoted by Croce in *La filosofia* from the last few paragraphs of the *New Science*.[45] Vico does not use "providence" in this passage, but it is to the mind of providence that he is referring. Vico says that the world of nations has been made by men themselves but that this world has issued from "a mind often diverse, at times quite contrary, and always superior to the particular ends that men had proposed for themselves; which narrow ends, made means to serve wider ends, it has always employed to preserve the human race upon this earth" (1108; compare 342, 344). Croce, in the conclusion to *La filosofia*, claims that Vico's providence, as the objective, logical order of history, is what Hegel formulated as the "cunning of reason" (*List der Vernunft*).[46] This claim is symptomatic of Croce's Hegelianizing of Vico. But to equate Vichian providence with nothing more than order in history is only to give a partial account, for Vico means that history truly has a divine order and is divinely directed.

Beckett is quite clear that Joyce adds a fourth age to the three ages—gods, heroes, and men—of Vico's *corso* and *ricorso* of ideal eternal history, that of providence.[47] This point is missed by some Joyce scholars who, not having read Vico, speak of Vico's four ages, presuming that Joyce's cycle is taken over directly from Vico. They have not only missed what Vico said, they have also missed what Beckett said. As Beckett states: "Part 4 is the day beginning again, and corresponds to Vico's Providence, or to the transition from the Human to the Theocratic, or to an abstraction—Generation. Mr. Joyce does not take birth for granted, as Vico seems to have done."[48] Joyce's "providentiality" is what holds together Vico's *corso* and *ricorso*. But Joyce's "providentiality," unlike Vico's, is wholly within history, and history is wholly within us.

Regarding the course and later recourse a nation undergoes, Beckett grasps Vico's sense of decline, which includes "a six-termed progression of motives: necessity, utility, convenience, pleasure, luxury, abuse of luxury."[49] Beckett is paraphrasing Vico's axiom 66 in the *New Science*: "Men first feel necessity, then look for utility, next attend to comfort, still later amuse themselves with pleasure, thence grow dissolute in luxury, and finally go mad and waste their substance [*finalmente impazzano in istrapazzar le sostanze*]" (241). Beckett says: "At this point Vico applies Bruno—though he takes very good care not to say so."[50] Change, for Vico and for Bruno, is a transformation of opposites. Vico cannot mention Bruno by name because Bruno is a heretic and the Inquisition was unofficially present in Naples.

Vico does mention Bruno indirectly but prominently in describing the proof that governs his *New Science*, claiming that the matters of his science "have been established by divine providence, the course of the things of the nations had to be, must now be, and will have to be [*dovettero, debbono e dovranno*] such as our Science demonstrates, even if infinite worlds were born from time to time through eternity, which is certainly not the case" (348). This is likely an endorsement of Bruno's doctrine, such as can be found in his *De l'infinito universo et mondi* (*On the Infinite Universe and Worlds*), emphasized by declaring that such is "certainly not the case." Vico's denial that there are infinite worlds is a means to suggest to the reader that there may be such. Otherwise, there is no need for Vico to raise the issue at all. Bruno can lead us to Vico, as Beckett's title implies, if we realize that Bruno's metaphysical doctrine of opposites can be assumed and transposed into a historical doctrine of ages, in which one age passes into another. They both are joined by Joyce in his "book of Doublends Jined" (20.15–16).

Reading Dante

In the last major point of his essay, Beckett instructs the reader in Joyce's use of language. It is obvious that all of the *Wake* is built upon wordplay, involving many languages, based on modifications of the spelling, syntax, and significance of everything on each page. These complexities are evident and pervasive. Beckett insists that the words do not refer to what they are about. Rather, the words become in the text what the words themselves are about. The linguistic act does not have its meaning in some separate act of perceiving the objects to which the words refer, but is the thing meant itself. Beckett points out that such semiotics are not unknown in literature. They can be found, for example, in passages of Shakespeare and in Dickens's *Great Expectations*, but only at certain moments. The difference between these texts and that of *Finnegans Wake* is that in it Joyce does not *sometimes* use words in this way—he uses words in *nothing but* this way. His work requires a new sense of reading, a new kind of reader.

Not only has Vico prepared the way for Joyce's sense of history, he also has prepared the way for Joyce's use of language. Vico causes the reader of the *New Science* constantly to consider the multiple and original meanings of the words that carry the content of his philosophy. He does this by using language hieroglyphically. Liselotte Dieckmann points out that *geroglifico* signifies, for Vico, more than it did as a mode of emblematic expression for writers in the early Renaissance. She concludes that "it can safely be stated that, while resuming a very old tradition, Vico filled it with new and interesting meanings hitherto unknown to the hieroglyphical writers."[51] We may add to Dieckmann's observation that of Mary T. Reynolds: "An idea begins its existence when it has been given a shape. Through the study of language, as Vico knew, we recover a past reality; Vico came to his understanding of language through Dante, and Joyce built *Finnegans Wake* on their combined insights."[52] Vico wrote hieroglyphically in the *New Science* as much as can be done while still keeping the forces of philosophical reason present.

When the *giganti* first apprehend the thunderous sky as Jove: "alzarono gli occhi ed avvertirono il cielo" ("they raise their eyes and become aware of the sky"), we feel their eyes raising in the words. In such a state they are "uomini tutti robuste forze di corpo, che, urlando, brontolando, spiegavano le loro violentissime passioni" ("men all robust bodily strength, who, shouting and grumbling, expressed their most violent passions") (377). Vico uses two very precise verbs: *urlare*, which is both the shout of a human and the howl of a beast, for the *giganti* are both, and *brontolare*, which is to grumble as a human reaction and to rumble (as of thunder). In these verbs we hear the violence of the passions themselves, and we also intellectually understand the theory of how they present the first human act.

Beckett draws a parallel between the Italian that Dante created in order to write the *Divina Commedia* and the English Joyce created in order to write *Work in Progress*. It is commonly said that Dante wrote in Florentine dialect, but Beckett points out that the Tuscan in which Dante writes was spoken by no one: "He did not write in Florentine anymore than Neapolitan. He wrote a vulgar that *could* have been spoken by an ideal Italian who had assimilated what was best in all the dialects of his country, but which in fact was certainly not spoken nor ever had been." Beckett adds, however, that whereas Dante's language derived from what was spoken, "no creature in heaven or earth ever spoke the language of '*Work in Progress*.'" But he adds: "It is reasonable to admit that an international phenomenon might be capable of speaking it."[53]

Reynolds supports this claim of Beckett and comments that "leaving aside the many arguable features of Joyce's book, this determination to force language into a new range is testimony to Joyce's most ambitious and deliberate imitation of Dante."[54] Dante's language is performative. In the famous line of the *Inferno*—"Lasciate ogne speranza, voi ch'intrate"—we feel the loss of hope directly; we do not apprehend it as simply a description of what Dante is seeing inscribed over the portal. "Abandon every hope, you who enter."

Reynolds calls attention to a report by Ettore Settanni, who met with Joyce regarding an Italian translation of two fragments of the Anna Livia Plurabelle chapter of the *Wake* and was bewildered by Joyce's use of language: "Joyce took a copy of the *Divine Comedy* and pointed out Dante's line, 'Papé Satàn, papé Satà aleppe!' [*Inferno* 7:1] 'May Father Dante forgive me,' he said, 'but I took this technique of deformation as my point of departure in trying to achieve a harmony that vanquishes our intelligence as music does.' "[55] In commenting on this line, Charles S. Singleton points to the interpretation that *papé* expresses a state of mind of astonishment and marvel, and it is said twice to express these states more strongly. *Aleppe* is a form of speech that expresses a state of pain.[56]

It would not have escaped Joyce that Vico connects *papé* with the origin of language in his exposition of "poetic logic." Vico says: "Human words were formed next from interjections, which are sounds articulated under the impetus of violent passions. In all languages these are monosyllables. Thus it is not beyond likelihood that, when wonder [*maraviglia*] had been awakened in men by the first thunderbolts, those interjections of Jove should give birth to one produced by the human voice: *pa!*; and that this should then be doubled: *pape!*" (448). Vico likely intended this to remind the reader of Dante's famous line, to emphasize not only the onomatopoeia but its connection with wonder.[57] It enters in Joyce's eighth thunder word, which begins with "Pappappappa—" (332.05). There are echoes of "pa" or "ba" in every one of the ten thunder words (in the ninth, "da," "damandamna") (414.19). The thunder word on the first page of the *Wake* begins with "bababa," echoing the word in Florentine dialect for father, "babbo" (3.15). Jove, as Vico says, is the first father, the father of both men and gods.

In his youth, Joyce's friends called him "the Dante of Dublin."[58] Reynolds remarks that "Joyce appreciated Dante's art in all its aspects. His humor presents Dante's characters and scenes with a robust vitality, and many of his incongruous transformations have the value of presenting Dante's realism as an important element of the poem's surface that is easily overlooked."[59] Dante's poem is a comedy in the sense that it has a happy ending. Joyce ends *Finnegans Wake* with a reference to the final canto of Dante's *Paradiso*: Dante writes, "thus in the wind, on the light leaves, the

Sibyl's oracle was lost" (33.65).[60] In Virgil's *Aeneid*, the Sibyl, whom Aeneas consults, writes verses on leaves, but when they are blown by the wind she does not care where they go and makes no effort to catch them. On the final page of the *Wake*, Joyce has: "My leaves have drifted from me. All. But one clings still. I'll bear it on me. To remind me of. Lff!" (628.06–7).

The reader returns, in Dante's *Paradiso*, not to the dark wood of error of the beginning but to a partial grasp of divine self-knowledge, that circles on itself through its own reflected light and which illuminates the human image within it. It is a partial grasp because Dante says "as is the geometer who wholly applies himself to measure the circle, and finds not, in pondering, the principle of which he is in need, such was I at that new sight" (33.133–36). The divine circle cannot be squared but the square can be circled. The circle, since Aristotle, is the divine motion, the perfect geometric figure.

In 1927, in an Easter postcard, Joyce wrote to Harriet Shaw Weaver: "I am making an engine with only one wheel. No spokes of course. The wheel is a perfect square. You see what I am driving at, don't you? I am awfully solemn about it, mind you, so you must not think it is a silly story about the mooks and the grapes. No it's a wheel, I tell the world. *And* it's all *square*."[61] The engine with one wheel and no spokes is the "wholemole millwheeling vicociclometer" that Joyce is making from the *Scienza nuova*. Joyce's wheel is not the three circles or *giri* of the Trinity of divine geometry. It is the great wheel of the engine of history that encloses the square of gods, heroes, humans, and providence—Joyce's transposition of Vico's ideal eternal history.

The reader emerges from the great night of the *Wake* to find the beginning again, having been wheeled in a great circle. As Umberto Eco points out: "It is not the case that the book finishes because it has begun in a certain way; rather, *Finnegans Wake* begins because it finishes in that way."[62] In fiction generally, time can be reversible; time can be subverted such that events can be causally connected, as though they were contemporary. This subversion of causal connection is evident to the reader. Joyce, however, passes beyond this fictional sense of manipulating time and causal order rooted in it.

As Eco says: "In the *Wake*, the co-presence of diverse historical identities arises because there exist precise structural and semantic conditions that deny the causal order to which we are accustomed."[63] The reader can circle the square of history's four ages and know history in the manner that only God can, as a single field of events coincident with each other not as a sequence of past, present, and future. Instead, all is connected to all, but not in the sense of identity such that all is one; rather in the sense of an infinity of varying patterns of events which show that every event is in fact the repetition of another. No two events are identical, yet no event is unconnected to the whole that is the others. Joyce's Vichian-inspired providence is a step beyond the divine order of Dante in which the divine circling of God is transcendent of the world.

Joyce's semiotics takes us to this literary metaphysics, developed from Vico's "poetic metaphysics" of Jove of the *New Science* (374–99). Although Beckett holds that an Italian speaker sufficiently attuned to the dialects combined by Dante to create his special language of the *Divine Comedy* could employ it, he holds, as mentioned above, that no one except an "international phenomenon" might speak the language of *Finnegans Wake*. "It is reasonable to admit that an international phenomenon might be capable of speaking it, just as in 1300 none but an inter-regional phenomenon could have spoken the language of the Divine Comedy."[64] Each Italian dialect is its own language, just as each Italian city is its own country, but they are all Italian in some interrelated sense.

Joyce's language is all human language, not just aspects of a language that can be formulated in a universal manner. As Eco puts it: "Joyce must have derived from Vico the need for a 'mental language common to all nations,' interpreting it in a personal way within the polyglotism of the *Wake*."[65] Joyce can speak it and we hear it in our "earsighted" reading of the *Wake*. But one wonders how it could be spoken beyond how Joyce has spoken it. In trying to do so we might become like Salvatore in *The Name of the Rose*, who "spoke all languages, and no language. Or, rather, he had invented for himself a language which used the sinews of the languages to which he had been exposed—and once I thought that his was, not the Adamic language that a happy mankind had spoken, all united by a single tongue from the origin of the world to the Tower of Babel, or one of the languages that arose after the dire event of their division, but precisely the Babelish language of the first day after the divine chastisement, the language of primeval confusion."[66] Salvatore takes words from one language to begin a sentence and concludes it with words from another. He speaks not one language but all languages, and none correctly. To take up Joycean "language" and not to become Salvatore would be the problem of Beckett's "international" speaker.

Beckett makes no particular mention of the sense in which Joyce's work is based on humor. It is comic, not in the sense that it has a happy ending but in the sense that it is built through jokes. Even Dante is grasped through a joke or pun on his name, one of the best in the *Wake*: "the divine comic Denti Alligator" (440.06), and combined with Goethe and Shakespeare: "I always think in a wordworth's of that primed favourite continental poet, Daunty, Gouty and Shopkeeper" (539.05–6). Napoleon said that England is a country of shopkeepers. Joyce gives us a knowledge, not of divine providence but of "devine previdence, (if you are looking for the bilder deep your ear on the movietone!)" (62.07–9). If you wish to have divine prevision, the evidence is in the past as reported in the pictures (*Bilder*, German) in the Movietone newsreels that used to be shown in British and American theaters before the feature film.

The past is the key to the future, which is a repeat of the past, as is the present. The ancients look to the art of the Muses, who could sing of what was, is, and is to come, as we look to the Movietone newsreels, in which we see in the present what has already happened, and which often show us the new improvements in our life that are to come. See also "Devine's Previdence" (325.01–2) and "Devine Foresygth" (290.10–11). Joyce's providence is not Christian providence, taking us to the end of history, the day of Resurrection. Joyce's providence is not teleological, it is circular, constantly resurrecting each event and making it a new beginning again—the human comedy as comic, always going back around itself. Joyce gives us "Acomedy of letters!" (425.24) that "moves in vicous cicles yet remews the same" (134.16–17).

For Joyce to consider *Finnegans Wake* as the making of a great joke is not to claim it cannot make a great truth; it can claim *in risu veritas*. In *The Name of the Rose* it is said of William: "I never understood when he was jesting. In my country, when you joke you say something and then you laugh very noisily, so everyone shares in the joke. But William laughed only when he said serious things, and remained very serious when he was presumably joking."[67]

Of Jorge, who had hidden from the world the second book of Aristotle's *Poetics*, on comedy, it is said that his face was "deformed by hatred of philosophy." People believed his words because of his grimness, his *tetraggine*, which seemed the look of truth. But Jorge feared the possibilities of the comic. William says: "Perhaps the mission of those who love mankind is to make people laugh at the truth, *to make truth laugh* [*fare ridere la verità*], because the only truth lies in learning to free ourselves from insane passion for the truth."[68] Joyce's great joke frees the soul from the grimness of language that states its meaning in monotone, and replaces it with a language that can tell the truth in every way possible, such that we ask ourselves, as mentioned previously in the preface, herein: "Are we speachin d'anglas landadge or are you sprakin sea Djoytsch?" (485.12–13). Or are we speaking Joyce?

The first figure in Beckett's title is of course not a philosopher but a poet. Dante's poem embodies the philosophy of Thomas Aquinas as it is shaped by the Scholastic worldview. Dante is a philosophical poet, as he is called by George Santayana in his *Three Philosophical Poets*, the other two being Lucretius and Goethe. In discussing Dante, Santayana says that philosophy, like music, is a more intense experience than what occurs in common life: "For this reason philosophy, when a poet is not mindless, enters inevitably into his poetry, since it has entered into his life. . . . Never before or since has a poet lived in so large a landscape as Dante."[69] This landscape, on Santayana's view, is founded in the tradition of Neoplatonism, coupled with the categories of Aristotelian moral philosophy.

Joyce's education took him through the world of Scholastic thought. In *A Portrait* is the well-known discussion of Thomistic aesthetics, concerning the three aspects of beauty—*integritas*, *consonantia*, and *claritas*. A favorite subject of discussion with his students in Trieste was Thomistic thought, which he could discuss in quite precise terms. In these discussions he declared that Thomas Aquinas was the greatest philosopher, greater than Kant, Schopenhauer, or Nietzsche because his reasoning was "like a sharp sword." Joyce said he read Thomas in Latin, a page a day.[70] But in a letter to Ezra Pound of November 8, 1927, while writing *Work in Progress*, responding to a query Pound had concerning a phrase in Aquinas and which Joyce was unable to locate, Joyce concluded: "These philosophical terms are such tricky bombs that I am shy of handling them, being afraid they may go off in my hand."[71]

Joyce shared Aquinas with Dante, but the *Wake* is not a delayed work of the Middle Ages. As Eco stresses: "Were *Finnegans Wake* an extension of the Middle Ages, then Joyce's refusal of his own medievalism in the first part of the book would be an illusion. Were this the case, he would have denied the Scholastic philosophy of his earlier works, only to take a step backward into the medievalism of pre-Carolingian rhetoric."[72] Offsetting Dante as the poet of Scholastic Thomism is Vico's description of Dante as the "Tuscan Homer."

In Vico's fragment concerning "the discovery of the true Dante" that reflects his discovery of the true Homer in the *New Science*, he declares that "the *Comedy* of Dante Alighieri is to be read on three counts: as a history of barbaric times in Italy, as the source of very beautiful ways of Tuscan speaking, and as an example of sublime poetry."[73] Regarding Dante's language, Vico says in a letter to Gherardo degli Angioli that "on account of such poverty of vernacular speech, Dante, in order to unfold his *Comedy*, had to assemble a language from those of all the peoples of Italy, in the same way that Homer had compiled his, using all those of Greece."[74] As Homer was not a philosopher, as Vico maintained, so Dante was not one either, although, as Homer was followed by the Greek philosophers, so Dante was followed by the Italian Renaissance Humanistic philosophers.

The philosophers must always go to school with the poets, and as Santayana says, the great poets are always philosophical. Joyce brings Dante together with Bruno and Vico, and the result, to use Eco's words is: "an enormous 'world theater,' a *clavis universalis* in which ideas are so arranged that the structure of the work results in a 'mirror' of the cosmos. Although philosophy maintains the 'whereof one cannot speak, thereof one must be silent' (L. Wittgenstein, *Tractatus Logico-Philosophicus*, 7), *Finnegans Wake* makes the proud claim to bend language to express 'everything.' "[75] The ability to say everything is the philosophical ideal of the complete speech and it is also the way in which we advance from litter, to letter, to literature.

Chapter 2

✦

Joyce's Philosophical Vocabulary

Ancients

The general arrangements for the Wake were made at the direction of Cusanus, Bruno, and Vico, but many other philosophers appear among the visitors. In some instances we notice them as mostly a pun on their name; for example, the several puns on Kierkegaard as churchyard or cemetery, or a pun on Nietzsche's nihilistic tendencies, "the Nichtian," or on Einstein as "a one stone" or "a stone." The puns are sometimes expanded to include characterizations of their personalities and philosophies, as brought forth in the remarks that follow. They appear in Joyce's text in no historical order, for on its world-stage of memory all of history is a circle of coincidences. Some appear several times and in various disguises. They offer us a new vocabulary. To identify these thinkers, I wish to pull them back and return them to their traditional order in the history of philosophy.

We might, to an extent, look at Joyce's inclusion of the philosophers in the *Wake* in terms of the lines of Thornton Wilder, in *The Skin of Our Teeth*, a play he wrote after reading *Finnegans Wake*, and under its influence. One of the figures in the third act proposes that as the hours of the night pass over our heads, each is to be connected to a great philosopher: "Eleven o'clock, for instance, is Aristotle. And nine o'clock is Spinoza. Like that. . . . it means that when people are asleep they have all those lovely thoughts, much better than when they're awake." It means that "just like the hours and stars go by over our heads at night, in the same way the ideas and thoughts of the great men are in the air around us all the time and they're working on us, even when we don't know it."[1]

There are more than sixty philosophers who attend the Wake (all of whom can be found listed in the Appendix, herein). Joyce's approach to philosophy, I think, is captured in the following saying, given to me many years ago by a waiter in an Italian restaurant: "La filosofia è quella materia, con la quale o senza la quale, si resta tale e quale" ("Philosophy is that subject, with which or without which, all remains just the same"). But in the meantime we can find it as part of the "grand funferall" (13.15), the "funforall" (458.22) of *Finnegans Wake*.

Among the first to arrive is Anaxagoras or "Inexagoras" (155.32–33), who was the first of the Presocratics to teach in Athens, where he influenced Pericles and Euripides. His Joycean name is a play on "inexact," from ανα (Greek) and *ana* (Latin), a negative prefix. Anaxagoras is accused of ambiguity in his view that "in everything there is a portion of everything."[2] He cannot account for qualitative change simply through this principle. He must have meant that in everything there is a portion of all the opposites, but the meaning is left unclear. Very probably he wrote only one book, but several others are attributed to him, including one on the squaring of the circle.[3] Of course everything is in everything, as Joyce's circle shows. In the passage cited above, Inexagoras is accompanied by "Niklaus" (of Cusa), the philosopher of *coincidentia oppositorum*, and "Orasmus" (of Rotterdam), the philosopher of *moria* or folly, by means of which human order is connected to its opposite, human folly, "to the extinction of Niklaus altogether . . . by Neuclidius and Inexagoras and Mumfsen and Thumpsem, by Orasmus" (155.31–33).

In the *Phaedo*, Socrates says he once heard someone reading from a book of Anaxagoras, and thought it held out great promise to explain the world as ordered by intelligence (*nous*), but on obtaining the work thought it disappointing: "It was a wonderful hope, my friend, but it was quickly dashed. As I read on I discovered a man who made no use of his Intelligence [there is a pun on *nous*] and assigned to it no responsibility for the order of the world, but adduced reasons like air and ether and water and many other oddities."[4] Anaxagoras failed to invoke his own theory of cosmic mind, and in so doing failed to use his own mind. Socrates proceeds to apply these causal oddities to himself, making a joke of them, turning himself into a pile of bones and sinews without a mind to be responsible for his actions. Inexagoras gets nothing right.

Socrates appears twice at the Wake, once in a list of ancient figures in the margin of the classbook section, and another time as "morphomelosophopancreates" (88.09), as the form of the melodious all-powerful *sophos* or sage, who solves the Cartesian problem of being sure of himself with his well-proportioned or musical thought. At the beginning of the *Phaedrus*, Socrates tells Phaedrus that he has no time to spend on the scientific interpretation of myth because he is devoted to the instruction of the Delphic oracle, to seek self-knowledge above all else, and he is sure that this is his mission.

Plato's presence in *Finnegans Wake* has been discussed in the introduction, but we may add a further observation. Joyce offers a solution to the famous problem, in Platonic metaphysics, concerning how particulars participate in the forms or *eidē*. The identity of any common class of particulars rests in the reality of the *eidos*, in which they can be said to participate, but it is problematic to say what this relationship of participation is. If we posit a third thing, which designates the connection between a particular and its form, we find ourselves in the predicament of the "third-man argument"—for we must now say how this synthetic factor is connected, both to the form on the one hand and to the particular on the other.

To solve this problem we require now two more things; one to connect the third thing to the form and another to connect it also to the particular, and so on, in an indefinite regress, which we are unable to sum. The sum of such a regress is a logical impossibility, a contradiction. Joyce resolves the question in a single stroke with his formulation of Plato's name, discussed earlier, showing that each of the letters connects to each other to form Plato's name, giving him his identity—"P.t.l.o.a.t.o." (286.03). Since Plato is a particular form made of particular letters, his identity (slightly modified) can be connected to many others in Joyce's process of resurrection.

Aristotle appears three times, once, by his correct name, in the margin of the classbook section, along with Socrates and Plato (306–7). He appears as "aboove his subject probably in Harrystotalies" (110.17). His subject was probably based on Tom, Dick, or Harry's—Socrates, Plato, or Aristotle's lies—or what he says lies in Aristotle. Aristotle appears a final time in the passage discussed in the introduction concerning the Ondt and the Gracehoper episode, in which the Ondt is seated and sated before his Platonic "plate o'monkynous and a confucion of minthe (for he was a conformed aceticist and aristotaller)" (417.15–16). Plato's metaphysical mind is joined to Aristotle's scientific mind through the sensible ethics of moderation of Confucius. Aristotle is a teetotaler whose "comfrotumble phullupsuppy" does not include what happens at events like Plato's drinking party of the *Symposium*.

Aristotle is also a "totaller." He is the first philosopher to write a treatise on every part of human knowledge to create the forms of all the sciences. As Goethe says: "Plato relates himself to the world as a blessed spirit, whom it pleases sometimes to stay for a while in the world. . . . Aristotle, on the contrary, stands to the world as a man, an architect. He is only here once and must here make and create. . . . He draws a huge circumference for his building, procures materials from all sides, arranges them, piles them up, and climbs them in regular form, pyramid fashion to the top; whereas Plato, like an obelisk, indeed like a pointed flame, seeks heaven."[5]

Cicero appears first as et cetera "etsitaraw etcicero. And you, Bruno Nowlan, take your tongue out of your inkpot!" (152.10–11). Cicero, the greatest Roman philosopher and orator, was famous for his eloquence, that especially emerged in his powerful digressions, in which he took his listeners down "long sizzleroads" (577.28) in order to bring them back in a flash to the issue at hand. Etc. and a number of other common Latin abbreviations, such as i.e., n.b., and e.g., known as *Notae Tironianae*, were invented by Cicero's slave and secretary, Tiro, who devised a shorthand to take down Cicero's words in court proceedings, and was the first to record verbatim a speech in the Senate. Bruno is reminded to take his tongue out of his inkpot and speak, because Bruno was famous for his eloquence. Philosophy requires eloquence. The truth cannot simply be pursued as flat statements on paper. Shaun, in speaking about speaking, declares: "'I'd perorate a chickerow'" (425.19). I'd imitate a Cicero, for Cicero is famous not only for his powerful digressions but also for his power of peroration, that is, his power of the conclusion to his forensic orations.

Cicero regards Socrates not as the enemy of rhetoric but as the greatest of philosophical rhetoricians, because he could not have taught as he did without his ability in eloquence. Cicero asks: "What of Critias? and Alcibiades? these though not benefactors of their fellow-citizens were undoubtedly learned and eloquent; and did they not owe their training to the discussions of Socrates?"[6] If Homer is the poet for all poets to imitate, Cicero is the orator for all orators to imitate. And Socrates is the philosopher for all philosophers to imitate, which means they, with Bruno, must not keep their tongues in their inkpots but must make language speak, not be simply silent on the page.

Medievals

The early medieval Irish ethicist, Pelagius, for whom the heresy of Pelagianism is named, appears several times. Pelagius denied the doctrines of divine grace and original sin, holding that through simply the proper exercise of free will, man can attain moral perfection. The aid of divine grace is not needed for morality. Against the doctrine of original sin, Pelagius firmly held that man is inherently good. We find ourselves "between Pelagios and little Chistayas" (538.36–539.01). We find ourselves between big Pelagius and little Christians, between standing on our own two feet, seeking perfection through our own free will, and standing humbly in need of grace to confront our fallen nature. Augustine, while calling him "a saintly man," was the formidable adversary of Pelagius.

Augustine, the bishop of Hippo, defended the doctrines of grace and original sin while also advocating the freedom of the will: "Ecclectiastes of Hippo outpuffs the writress of Havvah-ban-Annah—to pianissime a slightly varied version of Crookedribs confidentials" (38.29–31). *Hawah* (Hebrew), Eve says "have a banana" in a varied version of the story of the apple, connected to the Mohammedan varied version of Eve's creation out of a crooked rib of Adam. Pelagius is also "Pelagiarist!" (525.07), "prelaged" (358.10), and responsible for "how very many piously forged palimpsests slipped in the first place by this morbid process from his pelagiarist pen?" (182.02–3). Although Pelagius is author of an original doctrine of morality in relation to that of the Christian, it is a palimpsest of that already held by the Stoics.

Johannes Scotus Eriugena, or John the Irishman, "Eriugena" (of Erin) being a neologism invented by John himself as a way of stating his identity. "Scotus" also meant Irishman in the Latin of his period. He worked on the Continent, however, under the patronage of Charles the Bald. He was perceived as having Pelagian tendencies because of an overemphasis on human free will in his account of the conception of divine predestination. He arrives at the Wake in the company of the chief disciple of Pelagius, Caelestius, who was tried and excommunicated by the Council of Carthage in 411 for preaching the Pelagian doctrine: "erigenating from next to nothing and celescalating the himals and all, hierarchitectitiptitoploftical" (4.36–5.02).

Eriugena's cosmology, influenced by the Neoplatonic doctrine of nature as a series of emanations from the Godhead, was condemned for pantheism at Paris in 1210. His scheme in his masterwork, *On the Division of Nature*, distinguishes four kinds of nature. The Master says to his Disciple, at the beginning of this work: "It seems to me that nature is subdivided into four species or kinds by four differences or distinguishing marks: (1) a nature which creates but is not created; (2) a nature which creates and is created; (3) a nature which is created and does not create; (4) a nature which neither creates nor is created."[7] The first kind of nature is God, the second are archetypes existing in the divine mind, the third are the creatures of the visible world existing outside the divine mind, and the fourth is God, as the end of the creative process in which all that is created is reunited in divine reality. The third are creatures that participate in God's reality but that are also created out of nothing (or perhaps "next to nothing").

Eriugena's scheme is "hierarchitectitiptitoploftical"—its hierarchical architecture is pontifical in its proliferation. "But Erigureen is ever" (279.03). But his scheme is over because no one is a Christian Neoplatonist today. "Juan delivered himself with express cordiality, marked by clearance of diction and general delivery, as he began to take leave of his scolastica at once so as to gain time with deep affection" (431.21–24). Eriugena, unlike the single-mindedness of Scholastic logicians, exploits the presence of multiple meanings in texts, and thus seems to take leave of his senses. His *Periphyseon* exploits his concept of polysemy through which he pursues etymologies of various words in accordance with the view that derives from the Stoics, that the study of the origins of words takes us back to a knowledge of the things the words represent. Eriugena has the Irish gift for gab, even creating his own flowery way of referring to himself. His philosophy is passed over, but like the Emerald Isle which he left for the Continent, his thoughts remain evergreen.

Saint Thomas Aquinas, born at Roccasecca near Naples, and studying there, is part of the trio of Neapolitans at the Wake, along with Bruno of Nola—the heretic, and Vico—the virtuous paganized Christian, born in via San Biagio dei Librai, the street of the booksellers, part of the system of streets called *Spaccanapoli* that split ancient Naples in two. A short distance away is the church in which Thomas is said to have spoken. Thomistic views run throughout Joyce's thinking, from his aesthetic theory, introduced in chapter 19 of *Stephen Hero* as "applied Aquinas," to its expanded formulation in *A Portrait*, to Stephen's incorporation of Thomistic methods of argument for his rebuttal in the ninth chapter of *Ulysses*. In *Finnegans Wake* Aquinas appears, not as the great wielder of the sharp mental sword of philosophical reasoning but as the embodied philosopher of great corpulence: "the latten stomach even of a tumass equinous" (93.09), having an iron stomach and big as a horse. He is "tunnibelly" (113.36), "With his tumescinquinance in the thight of his tumstull" (240.08–9).

In the third chapter of *Ulysses* appears "Aquinas tunbelly."[8] A tunbelly is a potbelly, and, even larger, a "tun" is a vessel as large as a beer or wine cask, "the whole stock company of the old house of the Leaking Barrel, was thomistically drunk" (510.17–18). Saint Thomas was, by medieval legend, so big-bellied that it was necessary to have dining tables cut out to fit around his stomach.

In the same line in *Ulysses* Aquinas is called "*frate porcospino*," the "porcupine Monk" or literally "brother porcupine," which may allude to the prickly power of his arguments. The Italian *porcospino* is composed of "*porco*" (pig) and "*spino*" (thorn), a prickly pig. It has the figurative meaning of a person who is brusque and closed in relation to others. Aquinas was not only unusually large, he was unusually quiet in his manner—by tradition reported to have been called "the dumb ox" by his fellow students. His teacher, Albert the Great, however, declared: "We call him the dumb ox, but in his teaching he will one day produce such a bellowing that it will be heard throughout the world." It was difficult to make his "arrahquinonthiance" (296.20); "Please by acquiester to meek my acquointance!" (145.10); "Yet an I saw a sign of him, if you could scrape out his acquinntence?" (514.16–17). Aquinas the human figure was as difficult to approach as later was his thought to master. When he appears at the Wake, he looms large.

Moderns

We can pass into the Italian Renaissance with the two "Florentines"—the founder of modern politics, Niccolò Machiavelli, and the founder of modern physics, Galileo Galilei. Joyce asks: "The prince in principel should not expose his person? Machevuole!" (89.06–7). Machiavelli's *The Prince*, as is well known, concerns the methods and rules a prince must follow to manifest strength (*virtù*) and maintain his position in a particular state (*lo Stato*), the first principle of which is that the Prince not expose his real intention, which is simply to retain power. Thus Machiavelli redefines *virtù* from those cardinal virtues that Ciceronian and Christian versions of the wise ruler are supposed to embody.

For, Machiavelli writes: "many have fancied for themselves republics and principalities that have never been seen or known to exist in reality. For there is such a difference between how men live and how they ought to live that he who abandons what is done for what ought to be done learns his destruction rather than his preservation, because any man who under all conditions insists on making it his business to be good will surely be destroyed among so many who are not good. Hence a prince, in order to hold his position, must acquire the power to be not good, and understand when to use it and when not to use it, in accord with necessity."[9] The answer to the question posed in Italian is "*Ma che vuole*?" or "But what do you expect?" or "But what do you want?"

To condemn a form of political thought it is enough to portray it as Machiavellian. It is enough for Shem, who is always writing "inartistic portraits of himself," to present himself "in the act of reciting old Nichiabelli's monolook interyerear *Hanno, o Nonanno, acce'l brubblemm'* as, ser Autore, q.e.d." (182.19–21). Machiavelli is evil (Old Nick, Niccolò), seeing the State as a form of internal warfare (*bellum*). Political power is a matter of "*hanno o non hanno*" (they have or have not) power. The author demonstrates (Q.E.D.) that the problem of the prince is "To be, or not to be; that is the question" (Hamlet 3.1.58) = "*Essere o non essere, questo è il problema*." It is also necessary to accept (*accettare*) that this is the problem.

Machiavelli and Galileo appear together: "Turning up and fingering over the most dantellising peaches in the lingerous longerous book of the dark. Look at this passage about Galilleotto. I know it is difficult but when your goche I go dead. Turn now to this patch upon Smachiavelluti. Soot allours, he's sure to spot it" (251.23–26). The stars are viewed by both Dante and Galileo. These are the stars that Dante sees from the dark wood of the first canto of the *Inferno*: "the sun was mounting with the stars that were with it when Divine Love first set those beautiful things in motion."[10] They are signs of the divine like the "delectable mountain" (*dilettoso monte*) that holds his vision when he encounters Virgil.[11] In his book of the night, *The Starry Messenger* (*Sidereus Nuncius*), Galileo writes: "When stars are viewed by means of unaided natural vision, they present themselves to us not as of their simple (and, so to speak, their physical) size, but as irradiated by a certain fulgor and as fringed with sparkling rays, especially when the night is far advanced."[12]

"Smacchiavelluti," the clean (*smacchia*) velvet (*velluto*) is what Machiavelli dons while composing, at night, his book of the dark forces of gaining and holding power—*The Prince*. Machiavelli writes, in his famous letter to Francesco Vettori, his benefactor in Rome, while exiled at his farm outside Florence: "On the coming of evening, I return to my house and enter my study; and at the door I take off the day's clothing, covered with mud and dust, and put on garments regal and courtly; and reclothed appropriately, I enter the ancient courts of ancient men. . . . And because Dante says it does not produce knowledge when we hear but do not remember, I have noted everything in their conversation which has profited me, and have composed a little work *On Princedoms*."[13] Machiavelli is dressed in a princely manner, in regal velvet. What is regal in Italian is *principesco*. Velvet may have also a resonance with the method of the prince, to rule by "*il pugno di ferro e guanto di velluto*" ("an iron first in a velvet glove").

Machiavelli, like Galileo, is a "go-between." Galeotto is Gallehault, who in King Arthur's court arranged the union between Lancelot and Queen Guinevere, and whose name ("Galeotto"),[14] like Pandarus ("pander"), who procured for Troilus the love of Cressida in Chaucer's poem, became a synonym for "go-between." Galileo is the *galeotto* for the union of the starry heavens and the earth and Machiavelli is the same between the prince and those the prince rules. Both Machiavelli and Galileo end their careers at odds with the authorities, the state and the church, in effect under house arrest in properties outside the city of Florence.

Francis Bacon appears several times at the Wake as bacon and eggs: "auld Daddy Deacon who could stow well his place of beacon" and "illed Diddiddy Achin for the prize of a pease of bakin with a pinch of the panch of the ponch in jurys for" (257.14–15, 21–23). "Like old Dolldy Icon when he cooked up his iggs in bicon" (339.03–4); "till that hen of Kaven's shows her beaconegg" (382.10–11); "with a second course eyer and becon" (406.15); "like a grace of beckoning over his egglips" (603.01–2); "after their dinners of cheeckin and beggin" (205.18–19). Bacon, the founder of the new logic of induction and experimentation, died by his own science, on Easter day, from a chill he caught after stopping his carriage to procure snow to pack into a chicken to see whether it would act as a preservative.

Bacon's approach to the hen was in accord with his principle that "*Natura einim non nisi parendo vincitur*"—"Nature to be commanded must be obeyed."[15] The purpose of knowledge is to understand nature in order to master it for our own purposes. The hen, for Bacon, the scientist and logician, is food, a medium of consumption or simply a part of biology, in contrast to the hen of the *Wake*, that unearths the letter from the midden heap and represents Anna Livia Plurabelle, symbolizing the feminine force of creativity. This hen survived Bacon's freezing experiment: "About that original hen. Midwinter (fruur or kuur?) was in the offing and Premver a promise of a pril when, as kischabrigies sang life's old sahatsong, an iceclad shiverer, merest of bantlings observed a cold fowl behaviourising strangely on that fatal midden" (110.22–25).

There are also some echoes of Bacon's having ended his career by using his opportunity, as attorney general and lord chancellor, to supplement his income, by taking payments from those whose cases he heard, and so being arrested and deprived of office by James I. Old Daddy Deacon "could stow well his place of beacon" and didn't he ache for the prize of a "pinch of the panch of the ponch!" Bacon was living high on the hog and off the fat of the land.

As mentioned earlier, Socrates arrives at the Wake having already surmounted the Cartesian problem of the self with his musical *elenchos* moving him toward self-knowledge. But Descartes, the modern Socrates, has his own version of the self—the *sum* of the *cogito*. Socrates was a master of uncertainty and of instilling it in others. Descartes was a master of certainty, inviting others to confirm it for themselves. "That he was only too cognitively conatively cogitabundantly sure of it because, living, loving, breathing and sleeping morphomelosophopancreates, as he most significantly did, whenever he thought he heard he saw he felt he made a bell clipperclipperclipperclipper" (88.07–11).

In his *Meditations on First Philosophy* (cogitabund: meditative), Descartes presents his method of hypothetical doubt by questioning whether his sensation of external things can be trusted as providing a certain knowledge of them, or even of their existence. He concludes that no such certainty is possible because the senses have deceived him in the past and thus may be deceiving him at any given moment. He then asks whether his internal sense, his sense of whether he is now asleep or awake, can be trusted. He concludes that at any time, no matter how vivid the feeling of being awake, he cannot be certain that he is. He could be dreaming. Thus, "whenever he thought he heard he saw he felt he made a bell clipperclipperclipperclipper." He clipped away at every sensation, external or internal, sounding the alarm of uncertainty.

Finally, Descartes asks whether he can be certain of mathematical truths because they seem the model of certainty: "For whether I am awake or asleep, two and three added together are five, and a square has no more than four sides. It seems impossible that such transparent truths should incur my suspicion of being false."[16] But: "Whether he was practically sure too of his lugs and truies names in this king and blouseman business? That he was pediculously so. Certified? As cad could be. Be lying!" (88.11–13).

Descartes decides, however, that even such truths are uncertain because it is possible that a "malicious deceiver" could exist, an anti-god as powerful as the Diety—the ultimate cad who could make such seemingly certain truths actually be lies. These doubts led Descartes to "be the lonee I will" (88.13–14). He can only be certain he exists as the one deceived. As long as he is a thinking I, *cogito ergo sum*, "I am, I exist." "But what then am I? A thing that thinks. What is that? A thing that doubts, understands, affirms, denies, is willing, is unwilling, and also imagines and has sensory perceptions."[17] Part of "I exist" is that "I will." The self is "reborn of the cards" (304.27–28) by means of the "Cartesian spring!" (301.25).

For Descartes: "singing glory allaloserem, cog it out, here goes a sum. So read we in must book. It tells. He prophets most who bilks the best" (304.31–305.02). In Anglo-Irish: "you cogged that sum"—you cribbed that sum. And, in fact, Descartes did; he cribbed it from Saint Augustine's "*si fallor, sum.*" This "cribbing" was called to Descartes's attention by one of his correspondents, and in a letter of November 14, 1640, he wrote in reply: "I am obliged to you for drawing my attention to the passage of

St. Augustine relevant to my *I am thinking, therefore I exist.* I went today to the library of this town [Leiden] to read it, and do indeed find that he does use it to prove the certainty of our existence."[18]

Vico, having found another precedent for Descartes's cogito in Plautus's comedy *Amphitryo*, in Sosia the slave's speech to prove his own identity, reports it in his *De antiquissima Italorum sapientia*, a work to which Joyce makes reference (287.23–25).[19] Descartes is the consummate philosophical comedian, never departing from the declaration in his early writings (*Cogitationes Privatae*) that he comes forth on the stage of the world like comedians do, in a mask.[20] As Vico remarks in the *Antiquissima*, the cogito is hardly a profound philosophical proposition, as anyone could utter it. As Descartes says in the first sentence of the *Discourse*, *bon sens* is the best distributed thing in the world, so much so that no one ever feels the need to acquire more of it.[21] Descartes's philosophy, based on understanding by the light of nature, always looks on the bright side. He always bilks the best.

George Berkeley, the Irish philosopher and Anglican bishop of Cloyne, born at Kilkenny, arrives with a bump, "the Burkley bump" (312.29). The bump is Dr. Johnson's famous attempt, by kicking a stone, to refute Berkeley's immaterialist metaphysics that maintains that to be (*esse*) is to be perceived (*percipi*). For if, as Berkeley said, stones had no "material substance" and were in fact just collections of "ideas," a shoe should pass right through one, without resistance. Johnson claimed to be on the side of common sense, but so did Berkeley, who claimed that to have common sense is to trust our senses.

Berkeley held his views to be in agreement with our ordinary views of the world, which cause us to believe that what we immediately perceive are the real things. In his *Philosophical Commentaries* (his notebooks) he remarked that the view that things in themselves are separate from what we sense of them, such that "the Wall is not white, the fire is not hot" is one he could not accept. He comments: "We Irish men cannot attain to these truths."[22] Things are not simply there but are there as objects of perception, having a relation to the mind. Berkeley is an idealist but not a solipsist, because things do not come in and out of existence relative to our perception of them. Their being is independent of our being but not of God's, who perceives all things at all times. All things are always in the mind of God and God is immaterial.

Berkeley's philosophy begins in his *An Essay on a New Theory of Vision*, in which he criticizes the geometric conception of seeing in Descartes's *Dioptrics*, holding that distance is not achieved by the convergence of angles of the object seen but is suggested by what is seen, which has a contingent, not a necessary relation to us. Secondary qualities such as the color of an object depend upon the light in which we see it. Things appear differently at midday than they do at dusk. Primary qualities such as the size and shape of an object vary according to our distance from it and angle of sight. "Balkelly" (611.05) has "all too many much illusiones though photoprismic velamina of hueful panepiphanal world spectacurum" (611.12–14).

Berkeley described the things of the world as "furniture of earth," that is, "zoantholitic furniture, from mineral through vegetal to animal, not appear to full up together fallen man than under but one photoreflection of the several iridals gradationes of solar light, that one which that part of it (furnit of heupanepi world) had shown itself (part of fur of huepanwor) unable to absorbere" (611.14–19). Berkeley's idealism is one of what is seen is what there is. Unlike Kant's idealism, there is no thing-in-itself, not even the self is a thing-in-itself: "the Ding hvad in idself id est, all objects (of panepiwor) allside showed themselves in trues coloribus" (611.21–23). The mind is not the id, nor, as Berkeley says, is it the brain, for the brain is an idea in the mind that the mind has of itself, based on its perception.

Berkeley's last philosophical work is one of the most curious in the history of philosophy: *A Chain of Philosophical Reflexions and Inquiries concerning the Virtues of Tar-Water, and Divers Other Subjects Connected Together and Arising from One Another*—later known by the title of its second edition: *Siris*. Much of the book is concerned with the merits and consumption of tar water as a cure-all, but it also carries on the theme of divine activity as the ultimate cause of phenomena. "*Muta*: Suc? He quoffs. Wutt? *Juva*: Sec! Wartar watar! Wett" (610.19–20). The exchange between *Muta* and *Juva* also has elements of Berkeley's most widely read presentation of his philosophy: *Three Dialogues between Hylas and Philonous*. The exchange begins, like Berkeley's first dialogue, with the "risen sun" (609.20), the purpose of which is "The while we, we are waiting, we are waiting for. Hymn" (609.22–23).

The purpose of the *Dialogues* is to combat skepticism and paradoxes, which Hylas the materialist promotes by the pursuit of divine reason, and the reality of mind that Philonous represents. "*Muta*: So that when we shall have acquired unification we shall pass on to diversity and when we shall have passed on to diversity we shall have acquired the instinct to combat and when we shall have acquired the instinct of combat we shall pass back to the spirit of appeasement? *Juva*: by the light of the bright reason which daysends to us from the high" (610.23–29).

Berkeley knows that much of philosophy is silly and against common sense. As he says in his preface to the *Dialogues*: "Upon the common principles of philosophers, we are not assured of the existence of things from their being perceived. And we are taught to distinguish their real nature from that which falls under our senses." Thus: "We spend our lives in doubting of those things which other men evidently know, and believing those things which they laugh at, and despise."[23] These are "the phyllisophies of Bussup Bulkeley" (435.10–11). As *Juva* says: "Bulkily, and he is fundementially theosophagusted over the whorse proceedings" (610.01–2). "Balkelly, archdruid of islish" (611.05) from Kilkenny, as it turns out, has a sense of humor.[24]

The representatives of German Idealism, Immanuel Kant and G. W. F. Hegel, arrive with hints at some little-known facts about their interests outside philosophy and comments about the reading of their works. "This battering babel allower the door and sideposts, he always said, was not the very remotest like the belzey babble of a bottle of boose which would not rouse him out o'slumber but reminded him loads more of the martiallawsey marses of foreign musikants' instrumongs" (64.09–14). Kant was the picture of self-control, such that it was said that his life moved like the most regular of regular verbs, so it was not booze which would rouse him from his dogmatic slumber under the spell of Christian Wolff's metaphysics. Kant said it was Hume who roused him out of his dogmatic slumber and led him to the realization that experience could not be composed of sense-impressions alone but required the mind to be in possession of synthetic a priori principles by which sense could be formed in the sensible (*Sinn im Sinnlichkeit*). This awakening led him to the first *Critique*, in the preface of which he declared: "Our age is, in especial degree, the age of critique, and to critique everything must submit."[25]

When later he extended critique to cover aesthetic judgment and art, it emerged that his preference in music was for military marches. In Königsberg there was little great art to experience, and Kant never left the city and its province. The University of Königsberg was described by Crown Prince Frederick on a visit there as "better suited to the training of bears than to becoming a theatre of the sciences." Thus we may say "tantoo pooveroo quant" (416.13) (Italian *tanto povero quanto*, "as poor as Kant"). Thus Kant lived a quiet, rather ordinary life, "Luckily there is another cant to the questy. Has any fellow, of the dime a dozen type, it might with some profit some dull evening quietly be hinted" (109.01–3). Kant's dinner companions often included the town sheriff. Late in his life he studied the local death notices in order to calculate his own life expectancy. Kant never married, saying that when he was young enough for a wife he could not afford one and when he could afford one he no longer had need of one.

How should we approach Kant's works in order to benefit our own thought? "Strike up a nodding acquaintance for our doctrine with the works of old Mrs Trot, senior, and Manoel Canter, junior, and Loper de Figas, nates maximum" (440.15–18). It is best to read Immanuel Kant along with the plays of the Spanish writer Lope Felix de Vega. *Figa* in Italian (an alternative spelling of *fica*, literally "fig") is cunt, which sounds very like Kant's name when it is pronounced in German. The problem with Kant's philosophy is to get some life into it.

Georg Wilhelm Frederich Hegel appears as "hegelstomes" (416.33). Hegel has a little-known connection to stones and minerals. On publishing his first book, *Phänomenologie des Geistes* (*Phenomenology of Spirit*), Hegel identified himself on the title page as "Dr. and Professor of Philosophy at Jena, Associate of the Jena Ducal Mineralogical Society." He became an "assessor" in the Society, and received a pass from the University of Jena for a field trip to Göttingen and the Harz Mountains for geological study. Hegel, the rockhound.

Hegel, the first phenomenologist, is also the practicing mineralogist. Perhaps identifying himself as a mineralogist is an enormous joke—the first of Hegel's many careful ironies—placed in the first book of his career, expected to be overlooked, as indeed it has been. When he lectured at Jena, Hegel was described as having an "odd smile," behind which was benevolence; yet there was something "sharp" and "ironic" about it. Like a poet and an ironist, Hegel never let anything go to waste.

The *Phenomenology* is widely regarded as the most difficult book to read in the history of philosophy, followed next by Kant's first *Critique*. The philosopher A. N. Whitehead, himself the author of a nearly unreadable book, *Process and Reality*, when once asked if he had read Hegel, replied that he had begun the *Phenomenology* but given up a short way into its preface. Thus, "Say, baroun lousadoor, who in hallhagal wrote the durn thing anyhow? Erect, beseated, mountback, against a partywall, below freezigrade, by the use of quill or style, with turbid or pellucid mind, accompanied or the reverse by mastication, interrupted by visit of seer to scribe or of scribe to site, atwixt two showers or atosst of a trike, rained upon or blown around, by a rightdown regular racer from the soil or by a too pained whittlewit laden with the loot of learning?" (107.36–108.07).

This book is a "loot of learning" because it declares "*Das Wahre ist das Ganze*"—"the True is the whole." Nothing is left out; it is a book of wisdom, a complete speech arriving finally at absolute knowing (*absolutes Wissen*). Hegel's huge system takes us by storm. It is a hailstorm of ideas, all connected to each other. It is ordered in twos or pairs, such as a party wall, a wall between two properties, to the use of which each occupier has a partial right. Hegel's whole is composed of a dialectic of opposites, each of which passes into the other and each of which completes the partial truth of the other. The dialectic is Hegel's "too painec whittlewit." Hegel's wit is what carries the book along.[26]

Coming to the end of his chapter on phrenology, craniology, *Schädelwissenschaft*, or *Schädellehre*, Hegel dismisses it by saying it equates the mind with a bone (reading the bumps on the skull), and its science is no different than when nature naively joins the organ of its highest function, the organ of generation (*Zeugung*), with the organ of *Pissen*, making a pun on *Wissen* (to know). Although consciousness is presented in the *Phenomenology* as traveling the highway of despair in search of absolute knowing, encountering illusion after illusion yet being resurrected at each stage, the book, like the *Wake* itself, is "lots of fun." As Bertholt Brecht said, Hegel "had the stuff of one of the greatest humorists among philosophers," and that he had "never met a person without a sense of humor who has understood Hegel's dialectic."[27]

Finally, we may note that Sigmund Freud and C. G. Jung are at the Wake. They are not philosophers as such but their theories have had significant influence on the modern conceptions of mind and the self. They are not exactly welcome guests—except that they provide some further fun. They form a pair, as "Tung-Toyd" (123.20); "but we grisly old Sykos who have done our unsmiling bit on 'alices, when they were yung and easily freudened, in the penumbra of the procuring room (and what oracular comepression we have had, very priveetly, of course, to apply to them!)[28] . . . what an innocent allabroad's adverb such as Michaelly looks like can be suggestive of under the pudendascope" (115. 21–30). Freud is "fraudstuff" (7.13), "the fraid born fraud diddled even death" (172.21), "agricolous manufraudurers" (173.16–17), and "Jungfraud's Messongebook" (460.20–21). Jung's theory of the "collective unconscious" takes us back to the beginning of mind.[29] Freud claims to have a science of the personal unconsciousness.[30] Psychoanalysis would purport to solve the central problem of philosophy—its raison d'être—the acquisition of self-knowledge, but it may just make us "Tung-Toyd."

Joyce's wordplays in regard to Freud and Jung take on a biting quality. His jokes are rejections of psychoanalysis. In a letter to Harriet Shaw Weaver from Zurich in June 1921, Joyce writes of "a certain Doctor Jung (the Swiss Tweedledum who is not to be confused with the Viennese Tweedledee Dr Freud)."[31] Psychoanalysis is a science that claims to interpret the logic of dreams and to allow us to enter the whole of the night world of the unconscious. It engages in the analysis of our stream-of-consciousness use of language to reveal the interior dialogue of the human self.

The world of the dream, of the unconscious, the language of interiorization is precisely the subject of *Finnegans Wake*. Joyce enters this part of the self through the joke, the pun—the penman is the pun man, the fun man. Freud writes a treatise on *Jokes and Their Relation to the Unconscious* and isolates a special kind of joke that he says is the most numerous: "They are the kind which are generally known as '*Kalauer*' ('*calembourgs*') [puns] and which pass as the lowest form of verbal joke, probably because they are the 'cheapest'—can be made with the least trouble."[32] Joyce's sense of the pun is not that of the *Kalauer* but of the *Wortspiel*. But Freud's approach to the unconscious employs neither; it is dead serious in its analytic of the causal effects of the unconscious on our conscious acts and thoughts.

Of the review article Jung wrote on *Ulysses* in 1932, Joyce wrote: "Did you see Jung's article and his letter to me. He seems to have read *Ulysses* from first to last without one smile. The only thing to do in such a case is to change one's drink."[33] Without a sense of humor, Joyce's work is impenetrable; nothing can be done but "to change one's drink," that is, to develop a distraction. Joyce's response, as mentioned earlier, to the view that his method of literature was derived from psychoanalysis was: "People want to put me out of the church to which I don't belong. I have nothing to do with psychoanalysis."[34]

Joyce's position in regard to psychoanalysis is analogous to Hegel's position in regard to phrenology. Franz Joseph Gall (1758–1828), the founder of "phrenology," was thought to be one of the greatest minds of his day, and was mourned after death as a great pioneer scientist. In exasperation regarding phrenology's merging of the mind with the skull, Hegel says: "The retort here would, strictly speaking, have to go the length of beating in the skull of anyone making such a judgement, in order to demonstrate in a manner just as palpable as his wisdom, that for a man, a bone is nothing *in itself*, much less *his* true reality.[35] "The skall of a gall" (364.14–15). Hegel must confront a false and fraudulent conception of consciousness widespread in the nineteenth century with his phenomenology of mind, as Joyce must confront a false and fraudulent conception of the unconscious based on the claim of a new science of the interior monologue that was widespread in the twentieth century. If Joyce were simply putting psychoanalytic stream of consciousness into literary form, the originality of *Finnegans Wake* would be not only compromised but trivialized, and itself a "freudful mistake" (411.35–36).

Why are Joyce's characterizations of these philosophies important? Through them, reason returns to the logic of the dream and the unconscious, from which reason came. Reason reenters the world of the imagination and memory, which are governed by coincidence and metamorphosis. When we look through Joyce's presentations of philosophers at the Wake we see these figures through his attention to what's in a name—from Anaxagoras "Inaxagoras" to Eriugena "Erigureen" to Berkeley "Burklley bump." When we can connect some of Joyce's lines about these philosophers with what we may know of them, they enter our memory and imagination, not simply as historical placeholders of doctrines to be learned and submitted to critical examination and investigation but as whole and peculiar personalities, whose doctrines are placed in many perspectives, from which they can be apprehended. They are not thus reduced, or dismissed, but are enlivened so that they are lots of fun. We know them better, and would like to know them even better.

Chapter 3

✦

Bruno's Equals of Opposites and Cusanus's Learned Ignorants

Of Learned Ignorance

Adaline Glasheen states, in the entry for Nicholas of Cusa in the *Third Census of Finnegans Wake*: "To my knowledge no Joycean has yet read Nicholas of Cusa." She also states that to her knowledge no Joycean has read Bruno.[1] Joyce likely came to Cusanus through his interest in Bruno. In *Giordano Bruno*, the book Joyce discussed in his 1903 review, "The Bruno Philosophy," J. Lewis McIntyre presents a sketch of the philosophy of Cusanus, showing it as a significant source for Bruno's thought.[2] Bruno's conception of the infinite as well as his principle of the coincidence of contraries have their origin in Cusanus's famous little treatise, *De docta ignorantia*.

In the third dialogue of *On the Infinite Universe and Worlds*, Bruno quotes with great approval from *Of Learned Ignorance* regarding Cusanus's cosmological views, and concludes: "This honest Cusan hath known and understood much; he is indeed one of the most remarkably talented men who hath lived in our world."[3] In the fifth and concluding dialogue of *Cause, Principle and Unity*, Bruno employs mathematical diagrams that are like those employed by Cusanus in *Of Learned Ignorance* to symbolize his conception of the coincidence of the absolute maximum and the absolute minimum, such that the opposites of a curve and a straight line "coincide in the principle and the minimum, since (as the Cusan, the inventor of geometry's most beautiful secrets, divinely pointed out) what difference could you find between the minimum arc and the minimum chord? Furthermore, in the maximum what difference could you find between the infinite circle and the straight line?"[4] Finally, in the third dialogue of *The Expulsion of the Triumphant Beast*, Bruno has the speaker advocate that the problem of the squaring of the circle "be placed in the hands of the Cardinal of Cusa, so that he can see whether with this he can liberate the disturbed geometricians from that troublesome inquiry into the squaring of the circle."[5]

Here Bruno and Cusanus come together in Joyce's favorite mathematical problem, the squaring of the circle. Bruno thinks that Cusanus's method of the infinite extension of the basic geometric figures of straight line, triangle, circle, and square, showing them to tend to coincide, contains the solution to squaring the circle. Both Cusanus and Bruno claim they had discovered a method for squaring the circle, but they in fact did not. In 1882 Ferdinand von Lindemann, the German mathematician, showed the squaring of the circle to be impossible when he proved π to be a transcendental number.[6]

The circle is the divine figure, the most perfect figure, as Aristotle and the ancients held. It is associated with the movement of the heavenly bodies, and later with the angelic spheres. For Cusanus the circle is symbolic of God as such. The square is terrestrial, the four elements, four directions. To square the circle would be to accomplish the coincidence of these opposites and would be to achieve a divine knowledge or at least the true symbolization of such. Because of his doctrine of learned ignorance Cusanus, in his theism, need not actually produce the mathematics of the squaring of the circle; he need only have the square approach the circle infinitely. Only in God could the two coincide. But Bruno would prefer their coincidence in nature itself. Joyce, in a single stroke—reminiscent of Alexander the Great's solution to dealing with the knot of Gordius—solved the problem by declaring that, instead of squaring the circle, he "circled the square."

Cusanus and Bruno are themselves opposites. Cusanus, born in 1401, is the first modern philosopher, and Bruno, burned alive in 1600, is the last figure of the Renaissance. Cusanus was a priest, cardinal, bishop, and a member of the commission of Constantinople charged with the attempt to negotiate with the Eastern Church for reuniting with that of Rome. He wrote works to support traditional theism and proposed an orthodox Christology. Bruno entered the Dominican order at an early age. When, much later, he was accused of heresy, he abandoned the Dominican habit and wandered Europe. He wrote books on magic, was closely involved with Hermeticism, and accepted Copernican heliocentricity.

Cusanus was a Neoplatonist. His doctrine of learned ignorance is a Christian version of Socratic ignorance, through which ancient philosophy is formed. Socrates says in the *Apology* that he is wise in human things but denies any wisdom in divine things. Pythagoras, before him, coined the word *philosophos* and also claimed that only the gods are wise; he is only a friend and lover of wisdom. Socrates subscribes to this definition but adds to it that human wisdom is to know that what the human is, is not known, nor is the Good. Socrates learns this wisdom of ignorance by questioning the claims of wisdom made by his fellow citizens of Athens—the politicians, poets, orators, and craftsmen.

Cusanus begins modern philosophy with a negative theology based on the fact that we cannot know God. We know only through opposites, and in so doing we are always unable to make the opposites coincide. They can be known to coincide only from the standpoint of the divine mind. Human wisdom requires that we learn this difference of mind, that we learn our ignorance of the ultimate form of thought. This learned ignorance is a transformation of the Socratic *elenchos*, which is a logic of opposites that can never lead to their coincidence in a conclusion. Both Socratic ignorance and Cusanian ignorance are doctrines of self-knowledge in which the self confronts its own inability in principle to know itself.

The Socratic confrontation of opposites is done through language. The Cusanian confrontation is represented by geometric figures. Cusanus claims that these are not to be taken as literal representations of the divine but are symbolizations of the coincidence of the absolute maximum and absolute minimum. The use of mathematics by Cusanus is distinctively modern and anticipates the use of mathematics in the rationalist philosophies of Descartes, the discoverer of analytic geometry, Spinoza, with his geometric ethics, and Leibniz, with his ideal of a universal characteristic.[7] It is also analogous to the transformation from Aristotelian natural science, which is based on the subject-predicate structure of language and results in the description of natural processes, to Galilean natural science, which is based on mathematical formulas and results in the prediction of events.[8]

It is not enough simply to say that opposites in experience coincide, that one side of an opposition can pass into the other. Such principles have been asserted since the ancients—from Hesiod's account of the emergence of the opposites of the world out of Chaos, Heraclitus's famous assertion "that all things happen by Strife and Necessity," Empedocles's moving principle of Love and Strife, and Ovid's *Metamorphoses*, in which "God—or kindlier Nature—composed this strife; for he rent asunder land from sky, and sea from land, and separated the ethereal heavens from the dense atmosphere."[9] Our experience, like the world itself, is composed of opposites and their transformations into each other.

Cusanus wishes to demonstrate metaphysically that opposites, taken in their most absolute sense, coincide, and do so by necessity. Such demonstration will show that the coincidence of opposites is the divine order of the creation. He holds that the primary nature of the infinite is captured in the mathematical conception of a straight line being a line that can be indefinitely extended. Further, he claims that the curve of a circle, if expanded or contracted indefinitely, will continuously approach a straight line. The same may be asserted of the angles of a triangle. Cusanus says: "I maintain, therefore, that if there were an infinite line, it would be a straight line, a triangle, a circle, a sphere. And, likewise if there were an infinite sphere, it would be a circle, a triangle, and a line. And the same thing must be said about an infinite triangle and an infinite circle."[10] Thus *maximum absolutum* and *maximum contractum* are *coincidentia oppositorum* and if this is demonstrated as true of the nature of things, it is the basis of all order.

Cusanus wishes to show that God as infinite is not an opposite of the world as finite. If this were so, God would be one term of an opposition and God's being would not be truly unlimited but limited by the finitude of the world. The difference between God and world is not between finitude and infinitude but between the fact that in the world these two ultimate opposites, that constitute the principle of opposition itself, only approach their possible coincidence. But in God they coincide, although we cannot conceive it as such and so remain in a state of learned ignorance. Unlike the positive theology of Thomism, in which all positive predicates are attributable to God's nature by analogy, Cusanus's negative theology places us in a state of ignorance of the divine. But his new mathematically symbolized metaphysics may have proved too much. It is a short step from asserting that the coincidence of the absolute maximum and minimum is in God to asserting that this coincidence is true of nature as a whole, making it appear to provide the basis for a pantheistic metaphysics—which Cusanus certainly does not intend—but which Bruno was incorrectly said to hold.

Bruno is Joyce's real interest, and it is Bruno that Joyce connects to Vico. Yet Cusanus takes his place as a guest at the Wake. But: "I am not hereby giving my final endorsement to the learned ignorants of the Cusanus philosophism in which old Nicholas pegs it down that the smarter the spin of the top the sounder the span of the buttom. . . . And I shall be misunderstood if understood to give an unconditional sinequam to the heroicised furibouts of the Nolanus theory" (163.15–24). Nicholas of Cusa, the founder of modern metaphysics, coincides with Michael Cusack, the Irish nationalist and founder of the Gaelic Athletic Association: "Now let the centuple celves of my egourge as Micholas de Cusack calls them—of all of whose I in my hereinafter of course by recourse demission me—by the coincidance of their contraries reamalgamerge in that indentity of undiscernibles . . . this outandin brown candlestock melt Nolan's into peese!" (49.33–50.05).

The coincidence of contraries is "hypostaised by substintuation" (55.35–36). To hypostatize is to transform a conceptual entity so as to construe it as a self-subsistent substance, that is, to reify a concept. Cusanus reifies what he conceives into the actual order of substances. Furthermore, this reification has the sense of the theological hypostasis of the word as real and the biological sense of a hereditary character that is suppressed by epistasis and of the pairing of these contraries. Cusanus, then, gives metaphysical license to the pairing of all contraries and the appearance of "centuple celves." This pairing can happen by the Vichian *corso e ricorso* and by the Leibnizian "identity of indiscernibles," for no two entities that can be identified with each other are ever truly identical, or we could not even discern that they are two. Finally, the "undiscernibles" meet in Bruno's satire, *Il Candelaio* (*The Torch-Bearer*)—the Nolan's "candlestock."

The Cosmological Coincidence of Contraries

As Nikolaus von Kues or Nikolaus Kryfts, the German, was brought to Ireland through his coincidence with the Dubliner Micholas de Cusack, so Giordano Bruno, the Italian, is brought to Ireland through the Dublin bookseller Browne and Nolan.[11] Bruno Nolano, of Nola, is frequently referred to by Joyce as "the Nolan." This form of reference is not a Joycean creation; Bruno frequently called himself "the Nolan," perhaps to avoid the use of his monastic name, Giordano, which he took on entering the Dominican order to replace his baptismal name of Filippo. I. Frith's early book for "The English and Foreign Philosophical Library" was titled *Life of Giordano Bruno the Nolan* (1887), a work from which Joyce paraphrases a line in his article "The Day of the Rabblement" (1901).[12] Joyce, according to Beckett, puzzled his readers with the opening line: "No man, said the Nolan, can be a lover of the true or the good unless he abhors the multitude, and the artist, though he may employ the crowd, is very careful to isolate himself."[13] This echoes Ibsen's sentiment in *Et Vers*: "To live is to war with the trolls,"[14] a sentiment shared by Joyce.

In 1925 Joyce wrote to Harriet Shaw Weaver, telling her he would send her a "typescript of the first two watches of Mr Shaun" and explaining a number of references, including "Bruno Nolano (of Nola) another great southern Italian was quoted in my first pamphlet *The Day of the*

Rabblement. His philosophy is a kind of dualism—every power in nature must evoke an opposite in order to realize itself and opposition brings reunion etc. etc."[15] It is Bruno, not Cusanus, who prevails here, as Joyce places the coincidence of opposites in nature and not in the divine nature. In Browne and Nolan, Bruno the heretical philosopher is joined with an opposite philosopher, in that Peter Browne (1666–1735), an Irish bishop and fellow and provost of Trinity College, was a critic of Locke's theory of ideas, whose chief philosophical concern was to show how God can be analogically conceived by human beings.

The critical literature that gives any attention to Joyce's relation to Bruno largely repeats the same broad comment—that Joyce is influenced by Bruno's principle of the coincidence of contraries, and acts as though what this means is obvious—perhaps with the mention of a pair or pairs of opposites in the *Wake* to which it applies. But what is the logic of *coincidentia oppositorum*, that Bruno takes from Cusanus's metaphysics? I am using the terms "contraries" and "opposites" as synonymous. Logically, on the Traditional Square of Opposition, contrariety is a precise sense of opposition in which the two terms cannot both be true but can both be false—differing from contradictories, which cannot both be true, but also cannot both be false. In logical terms, the coincidence of contraries is perhaps best understood as the relation of "subcontraries," which cannot both be false and can both be true. Subcontraries can state partial truths that can be combined to make a distinction within the members of a given class.

In the fifth dialogue of *On the Infinite Universe and Worlds*, Philotheo, who speaks for Bruno, says: "You see further that our philosophy is by no means opposed to reason. It reduceth everything to a single origin and relateth everything to a single end, and maketh contraries to coincide, so that there is one primal foundation both of origin and of end." There is a single origin to everything—everything comes from an origin that is potentially everything (or, here comes everybody)—and thus the end of everything is already in the beginning—in the end is the beginning again; it "remews the same" (134.17). Philotheo concludes: "From this coincidence of contraries we deduce that ultimately it is divinely right to say and to hold that contraries are within contraries, wherefore it is not difficult to compass the knowledge that each thing is within every other."[16]

The movement from beginning to end is a macrocosm that holds within it as a receptacle multiple microcosms of the same movement of contraries that are less in scope than the two ultimate contraries that define the whole. Thus what is within the whole "moves in vicous cicles" (134.16). Implicit within Bruno's principle of contraries are the cycles of

Vico's "ideal eternal history." Only because the whole is an opposite of itself as beginning and end can there be coincidences of contraries within it which form all its particular contents. Bruno's cosmology provides a perfect pattern for the whole of human consciousness that is the subject of *Finnegans Wake*.

In the third dialogue of *Cause, Principle and Unity*, Teofilo says: "Hence, every potency, every act which, in the principle, is (so to speak) enfolded, united and unique, is unfolded, dispersed and multiplied in other things." Like the complete potency of the beginning and the complete and final act of the end, each specific entity is a constant circle of potency and act in which act becomes a new potency, making itself into a circle or cycle that passes continually beyond itself, always becoming what it is and what it is not. Thus what anything is, is also what it is not. No thing is sui generis.

This conception of a thing is a Brunian anticipation of the Hegelian principle of "determinate negation," namely, that what a thing is not always has content or is not merely null. As Teofilo continues: "The universe, which is the great simulacrum, the great image and sole-begotten nature, is also all that it can be, through the very species and principal members, and by containing the totality of matter to which nothing is added, nothing taken away, of complete and unified form." The universe is in a sense the one unique thing, the only true individual, in that it is complete in itself. But being complete, it is not perfect, because what it is, is constantly submerged in its particular processes of potency and act. Its internal motion can never complete itself. Its being is always a becoming. Thus Teofilo concludes: "But it is also not all that it can be, because of its very differences, its particulars, its modes and its individuals. It is only a shadow of the first act and the first potency, and, in consequence, potency and act are not absolutely one and the same thing in it, since none of its parts is all that it can be."[17]

The first act and first potency is the act of divine making as such, in which the two movements or contraries complete each other absolutely, without the medium of any particular refractions of its making. Nature is only a shadow of this absolute synthesis of potency and act. It imitates it in its own particular transformations of potency and act, but it is always in a state of becoming and can never cease its activity. The self-determination of the circle of the first potency and first act makes it be both equally still and in motion; its motion is a perfect stillness and its stillness is a perfect motion. Nature as a whole is like the divine nature but is not identical with it. Thus this is not pantheism. The divine is an opposite for nature but nature is not an opposite for the divine, because the divine is itself the perfect principle of potency and act on which nature depends for its self-identity. This conception of the self-contained infinity of the divine is an anticipation of the Hegelian "true infinity."

The problem of the relation of the finite to the infinite passes from the scheme of the four kinds of nature of John Scotus Eriugena through the Scholastics to Nicholas of Cusa, regarding the world and the human mind as finite and God as infinite. By endorsing Copernican astronomy Bruno brings infinity into created nature, asserting the universe to be infinite. It thus can have no center, but in it there are many world-systems that can have their own centers. Copernicus advanced a system in which the sun and the earth switch positions, but it remained for Bruno to draw out the implications of a total rearrangement of the solar system.[18]

Bruno holds that the celestial bodies that make up the universe have their own intrinsic principle of animation. As he states in the third dialogue of *The Ash Wednesday Supper*: "For, if we reflect, we will find that the earth and many other bodies, which are called stars and are the principal members of the universe, inasmuch as they give life and nourishment to the things which derive their substance from them and likewise give it back to them, they [the stars] must all the more so have life in themselves. By means of this life, they move according to an intrinsic principle toward the things and through the spaces appropriate to them, with an ordered and natural will."[19] In *On the Infinite Universe and Worlds* Bruno refers back to this point in *The Ash Wednesday Supper*, adding that all celestial bodies move "by the internal principle of their own soul" and "this earth doth from innate animal instinct, circle around her own centre in diverse fashion and around the sun."

Finally, Bruno asserts "that the Prime Origin is not that which moveth; but itself still and immobile it giveth the power to generate their own motion to an infinity of worlds."[20] These worlds, he says, are themselves great and small animals with their own patterns of mobility, each moving by its own nature. The product of infinite power must itself be infinite, but God as creator and maker is not identical with the created because, as the Prime Origin, God moves but in so doing remains unmoved. Bruno's metaphysics is not a pantheism but a theism that distinguishes the infinity of God's being from the infinity of worlds, which are each in themselves finite centers of animation. Bruno's metaphysics is very close to the formulation of a functional rather than a substantive conception of the interconnection of finite and infinite, such that the finite has an intrinsic principle of motion that allows it to replicate itself infinitely and determinately. The infinity of worlds is made possible by the coincidence of the contraries of finite and infinite.

Bruno's cosmology and metaphysics go well beyond his appearance in the *Wake*, yet the way Bruno thinks and his sense of things fascinated Joyce from the very beginning of his career, as can be seen not only in his use of the Nolan in "The Day of the Rabblement," criticizing the Irish theater, but from the fact that the stage name he chose in his late teens, when he thought of becoming an actor, was Gordon Brown—"a choice," Stanislaus Joyce reports, "which bore witness to his admiration for Giordano Bruno, whose philosophical essays he was reading at the time."[21] "Bruno" is "brown" in Italian and "Giordano" is "Jordan." "Gordon" is a Scots-Irish surname that can be used as a given name. Browne and Nolan are contraries, or more precisely subcontraries, as they are a twone—Bruno and Nolan are two but also one and the same. They correspond to Shem and Shaun, who are twins but also rivals. Shem is the penman; he is Bruno, who has taken his tongue out of the inkpot. Bruno's eloquence was so feared that at the *supplizio* of his martyrdom, according to the Vatican report, "his tongue was imprisoned" to prevent the populace from hearing his wicked words.[22]

Shaun is the postman, who is a fixed point around which Bruno moves—his birthplace, Nola, his constant point of reference as he wanders throughout northern Europe. "Mr 'Gladstone Browne' in the toll hut" (334.06–7). The British statesman W. E. Gladstone, in the tall hat, is also the source of the Gladstone bag, on which Joyce once gave an impromptu, detailed lecture to his language pupils. "Mr 'Bonaparte Nolan' under the natecup" (334.09–10), another displaced member of an Italian family, wearing his famous bicorne cap with its rump-like (*nates*) appearance, destined to conquer.

Joyce merges Bruno, his original philosopher of the pen, into Vico the post: "you mean Nolans but Volans" (488.15); "Nolans Volans" (558.18); "nolens volens" (Latin: "willing or unwilling," "willy-nilly"); "*a nuhlan the volkar*" (352.16–17); "*Til! Nolans go volants and Bruneyes come blue*" (418.31); "Mr. Browne, disguised as a vincentian, who, when seized of the facts, was overheard, in his secondary personality as a Nolan and underreared" (38.26–28). Throughout the *Wake*, however, Bruno remains the master of opposites, of movement: "alionola equal and opposite brunoipso" (488.09), even within his own identity, his "egobruno" (488.08), "Bruno at being eternally opposed by Nola" (488.10–11). Vico remains the master of the cycle whose movement is roundheaded, post-like, which is "whorled without aimed" (272.04–5) but which "annews" (277.18). "*Jordani et Jambaptistae mentibus revolvamus sapientiam*" (287.24–25).

We work our way back through the old, old story: "The olold stoliolum! From quiqui [French dialect: chicken, the hen] quinet [Edgar

Quinet] to michemiche chelet [Jules Michelet] and a jambebatiste to a brulobrulo! [to the burning of Bruno]. It is told in sounds in utter that, in signs so adds to, in universal, in polygluttural, in each auxiliary neutral idiom, sordomutics [deaf-mutes, Italian: *sordo*, deaf], florilingua, sheltafocal, flayflutter, a con's cubane, a pro's tutute, strassarab, ereperse and anythongue athall" (117.10–16). The old, old story is told in any tongue at all. The *Wake*, which takes us back to the language of the Vichian common mental language, tells the story in all languages at once, just as we are also taken back to the Italian philosophers of origin—the cosmology of Bruno and the ideal eternal history of Vico—pointed out to us, at present, by the scholars of the history of ideas, Quinet and Michelet.

The Expulsion of the Triumphant Beast

Joyce makes reference to Bruno's three ethical works: *Spaccio de la bestia trionfante; "Trionfante di bestia!"* (305.15); *Caballa del cavallo pegaseo con l'aggiunta dell'asino cillenico: "Nex quovis burro num fit mercaseus?"* (163.15) (*asino*, Italian; *burro*, Spanish = ass); *De gli eroici furori:* "the heroicised furibouts of the Nolanus theory" (163.23–24). These are all products of "the excellent Dr. Burroman" (163.34–35).

Although Bruno does not say so, *Spaccio de la bestia trionfante* (*The Expulsion of the Triumphant Beast*) is the argument Plato calls for in the tenth book of the *Republic*—for the poets or their supporters to make, to establish their right to have a place in the Socratic city. It is an instance of Bruno's general position of Neoplatonism. The poets, as the retellers of the myths, do not offer instruction in virtue but rather allow the gods and the heroes they portray to be guided by their passions and to act without restriction in both good and bad ways. Bruno's moral philosophy is presented as an account of how Jove expels the beings representing the vices from his heavenly realm and replaces them with classical mythical figures representing the virtues.

As Bruno puts it: "by placing in a certain number and order all of the first forms of morality, which are the capital virtues and vices, in such a manner that you will see introduced into the present work a repented Jove, whose heaven was full to overflowing with as many beasts as vices, according to the forms of forty-eight famous images [the constellations], a Jove now consulting about banishing them from heaven, from glory and a place of exaltation, destining for them, for the most part, certain regions on earth and allowing to succeed into those same seats the virtues, already for so long banished and undeservedly dispersed."[23] Bruno will accomplish these replacements by the Sun of the intellect.

Jove, "who represents each one of us," will be assisted by Momus, who in Bruno's account represents synderesis: "just as a man, in order to change his way of life and customs, is first invited by a certain light that resides in the crow's nest, topsail, or stern of our soul, which light is called synderesis by some, and here, perhaps is almost always signified by Momus."[24] Synderesis (Greek: *syntērēsis*, "preservation") is inborn knowledge of the primary principles of moral action. It enters Christian doctrine through Saint Jerome, to whom Thomas Aquinas refers in his discussion of conscience, in which he distinguishes between conscience and synderesis.[25] He regards synderesis as the grasp of the common and natural principles of moral order, and he regards conscience as the application of such knowledge to the particular and changing circumstances of life. The judgment of synderesis is universal in the sense that natural law is universal. Error is possible in applying these universal principles, but the principles themselves are not subject to error and these, in Bruno's terms, are illuminated by the Sun of the intellect.

Once Jove and the divine side we have in ourselves apply "the Sun of Intelligence and Light of Reason" to this problem, "then is expelled the triumphant beast, that is, the vices which predominate and are wont to tread upon the divine side."[26] In so doing the mind is purged of all errors and is adorned with all virtues. Bruno redefines the whole pantheon of gods, beginning by replacing the Bear, who held the most eminent part in heaven, with Truth. The form of reasoning that is required for the expulsion of the beast of vices and the establishment of figures of virtue to populate the heavens is made clear in the first dialogue by Sophia, who says: "What I wish to infer from that [the physical, mathematical, and moral oppositions in life] is that the beginning, the middle, and the end, the birth, the growth, and the perfection of all that we see, came from contraries, through contraries, into contraries, to contraries. And where there is contrariety, there is action and reaction, there is motion, there is diversity, there is number, there is order, there are degrees, there is succession, there is vicissitude."[27]

Metaphysics as well as morals depend solely upon this doctrine of thinking. The world of the *Wake* shows that consciousness itself proceeds in this way. Bruno sees all experience as a great wheel of movement. It is the engine with only one wheel, of which Joyce conceived when he was first thinking of the work that was to become *Finnegans Wake*—the engine that drives the wheel he found in Bruno's doctrine of contraries.

Cabala del cavallo pegaseo con l'aggiunta dell'asino cillenico (*Cabal of the Cheval Pegasus with Appendix on the Cillenican Ass*) contains a double pun built into the title by Bruno. "Cabala" suggests a horse, "cheval." The horse it suggests is the miraculous creature "Pegasus." "The doctrine of the coincidence of contraries equates this miraculous Cabal, comparable to Pegasus, the steed of the Muses, with the Cillenican ass that is none other than winged Mercury, who was born in a grotto on Mount Cillene."[28] "Asininity" is ignorance, and is a virtue. Bruno connects it with his scheme of the *Spaccio* by placing it in his reformed heaven. The human mind can have access to truth, either by ignorance and asininity or by science and knowledge. To claim any route to truth that falls intermediate between these two poles is to provide examples of foolishness.

Although Bruno does not say so, the ideal of asininity appears to be a transformation of Cusanus's doctrine of learned ignorance, for this doctrine keeps one from pretension to knowledge and the foolishness that results from such. Asininity allows one to be simply what one is. As a virtue it is an intellectual virtue that is also a moral virtue. As Bruno says: "the Ideal Ass is the productive, formative and supranaturally perfecting principle of the asinine species, which however much it is evident in the capacious bosom of Nature is distinct from other species. . . . As a matter of fact, it is from that species from which not only Asses, but men, stars, worlds, and terrestrial animals all depend: of that I say, in which there is no difference of form or subject, of things or things, but is simple and one."[29]

The Ass is the symbol of the first mind or universal One in which everything is equal. The Ass is the original species from which all emanate. As a moral ideal it is to act in accordance with the nature of things. To do otherwise, unless it is to act on the basis of true knowledge, is to engage in a form of foolishness. "You can ask your ass if he believes it" (20.26); "but I, poor ass, am but as their fourpart tinckler's dunkey" (405.06–7). "That folklore's straight from the ass his mouth" (480.06–7). By the coincidence of contraries, the lowest and humblest of the animals and of animal intelligence coincides with the highest and greatest.

De gli eroici furori (*The Heroic Frenzies*) treats of the relation between virtue and vice in terms of the coincidence of contraries. Instead of simply opposing virtue and vice it explains that one is derived from the other, through excess. In the second dialogue, Tansillo is asked why the distinction is not between the two terms as such. He replies: "Because both the contraries in excess—that is, in so far as they exceed—are vices, because they pass the line; and the same, in so far as they diminish, come to be virtues, because they are contained within limits."[30] He is asked further why virtue is not the other extreme from vice, and replies: "It is then in a state of virtue when it keeps to the middle, declining from one to the other opposite; but when it leads towards the extremes, inclining to one or the other of those, it fails so entirely from being virtue, that it is a double vice, which consists in this, that the thing recedes from its nature, the perfection of which consists in unity, and there where the opposites meet, its composition and virtue exist."[31]

In this conception of the relation of virtue and vice Bruno formulates a statement of Aristotle's doctrine of the mean or middle term (*to meson*) from the *Nicomachean Ethics* against his doctrine of the coincidence of contraries. If we take, for example, the virtue of liberality (*eleutheriotēs*) by expanding it in one direction to a maximum, the result is the vice of prodigality (*asōtia*), and extended in the other direction to a minimum, the result is the vice of stinginess (*aneleutheria*). Within virtue are the vices corresponding to it. There are no ethical means or middle terms for vices, only for virtues. The middle is the key to moral reasoning, as it is to reasoning in general. As Aristotle explains in the theory of the syllogism in the *Organon*, the middle term is the topos from which, on the one hand, the subject term can be drawn forth, and on the other the predicate, in order to being them together in the conclusion through the copula.

The wisdom needed to find the middle is prudence or *phronēsis*, which is an intellectual virtue. In the reformed order of the heavens in the *Spaccio*, Bruno has placed Prudence next to Truth, as for him the Search for Truth requires Prudence. Thus he states: "in order to be in proximity to Truth, Prudence is placed, with her maidens, Dialectic and Metaphysics; she has standing around on her right, Craftiness, Cunning, and Malice; on her left, Stupidity, Inertia, and Imprudence."[32] Bruno treats Prudence as a mean.

The wise, endowed with a heroic frenzy toward the truth, turn the inferior powers of the soul toward contemplation of the Supreme Intelligence. They "would be entirely lost, if there were not a certain conversion towards the splendor of intellectual things through the act of contemplation, by means of which they are converted from inferior degrees to superior ones."[33] The phenomenon of heroic frenzy is Bruno's solution to the problem Aristotle leaves unresolved in his ethics: how the best life, the life of contemplation, is to be integrated with *eudaimonia* as tied to moral action; how the opposites of *theōria*, which aims only at understanding sought as an end in itself, without regard for doing or making, and *phronēsis*, which is the power to choose the correct action and to perform it well, are to be reconciled.

The hero is not just the prudent actor. The hero's frenzy is for the truth itself that allows him to grasp the perfection of things. Since contraries are functions of each other, unlike substances, they can be complements.

Thus *theōria* and *phronēsis* are not two kinds of wisdom but are two extremes: the theoretical and the practical that comprise wisdom (*sophia*) itself. They form "the first heroic couplet from the fuguall tropical" (73.14–15). Wisdom is achieved by the middle, which acts as the topos or "tropical" from which both of its extremes can be drawn forth. The middle is both a topos and a tropical, a trope. The heroic frenzies are "heroticisms" (614.35). As Plato says in the *Cratylus*, all of the heroes are demigods because they sprang from the love of a god for a mortal, which is proved by the origin of the word in old Attic, "since it will show you that the name 'hero' [*hērōs*] is only a slightly altered form of the word 'love' [*erōs*]—the very thing from which the heroes sprang."[34]

Shem and Shaun

As noted earlier, Adaline Glasheen pointed out that to her knowledge no Joycean has read either Cusanus or Bruno. In regard to Cusanus, she further states that no one has "tried to work out the matter of twins as opposite and reconciled," and in regard to Bruno she adds that "Shem and Shaun are commonly said to illustrate his theory of the identity of opposites."[35] There are many pairings of opposites in *Finnegans Wake*, but that of Shem and Shaun is the archetype of Joyce's use of *coincidentia oppositorum*. There is no final way to comprehend the roles of Shem and Shaun and their exchange of places in the *Wake*. I wish to suggest one perspective that can be taken on their interconnection from the standpoint of Vico's conception of method in the *New Science*, as added to Bruno's conception of opposites.

Shem and Shaun are Irish for Jim and John, Joyce's and Vico's given names. Like Dante in the *Divine Comedy*, Joyce puts himself in *Finnegans Wake*. As Dante takes himself on his journey through the regions of the other world, Joyce, as Shem the penman, takes himself through the scenes of our night world, "Or dreamoneire"—"the book of Doublends Jined." Jim the Penman (associated with James Townshend Saward, the nineteenth-century English barrister and forger) can say anything he wishes, because he is a punman. Because "when men want to write letters" they are all "pen men, pun men," and such men are "fun men, hen men" (278.18–22). They turn litter into letter into literature. Perhaps we should "Shun the Punman!" (93.13).

"Shaun the Post" (206.11) is roundheaded, as Beckett calls Vico in his essay on *Work in Progress* (the Indo-European root for round, *rēt*, is "post," old English *rōd*, rod). Vico uses words in ways that play on their etymologies but he is not a pun maker; he accomplishes "cavileer grace by roundhered force" (465.16–17). Vico is "Johnny Post" (278.13), "misto posto" (Italian *allo stesso posto*, "in the same place") (430.10). Vico, like the reliable postman, makes his regular rounds in history. He is "Old Vico Roundpoint" (260.14–15). The "vicous cicles" (134.16) of his thought and words always "meet where terms begin" (452.22). Shaun the Post, like H.C.E., presents us with "his roundhead staple of other days" (4.34). He does not invent meanings but finds them, in history.

Joyce's method, as he explained it to Jacques Mercanton, was: "Chance furnishes me what I need. I am like a man who stumbles along; my foot strikes something. I bend over, and it is exactly what I want."[36] Joyce's method is that of the Muses. As we find in *Ulysses*: "Fabled by the daughters of memory. And yet it was in some way if not as memory fabled it."[37] The poet requires what the Muses offer by chance. *Finnegans Wake* is a prose poem, a theater of memory. The Muses sing of what was, is, and is to come. And as Hesiod says, they can sing many false songs, but can sing true ones when they will.

Vico's method, as he explained it in the *New Science*, is "indeed, we make bold to affirm that he who meditates this Science narrates to himself this ideal eternal history so far as he himself makes it for himself by that proof 'it had, has, and will have to be' ['*dovette, deve, dovrà*']" (349). The Muses always govern narration, for narration is to relate of something that was, is, and is to come. When narration is combined with meditation, this sequence becomes not one of simply before and after but a necessary sequence that brings forth how what was is presupposed by what is and what is to come presupposes what is. Philosophic narration, as distinguished from poetic narration, transforms the temporal art of the Muses into a logical art. We move from myth (the story) to logic (the account). When the Muses sing in a philosophic way they sing truly.

Jim the Penman has resurrected the *New Science* in our time, but to do so he has had to create a forgery of it, in which *corso* and *ricorso* are governed by chance and so become interchangeable and reversible. But a forgery is not nothing. It is what it is as a contrary to what is forged, the real original. It is what can pass for the original but is not. Once we know what the forgery is, we also know what the original is. The forgery is a false song because it is both true and false. It is a "false-truth." If it truly is a forgery it offers us by imitation the original, yet it is not the original. The joke is on us. But it takes us back to the original because if there were no original there could be no forgery of it.

Joyce's imagination is the product of chance but the result is not chaos. It is not nonsense because within *Finnegans Wake* is the original of the

New Science. Its roundheaded truth is what is being played upon. Shaun the Post is constantly delivering the ordered memory of the ages of ideal eternal history that are constantly being modified by Shem the Penman. Memory (Mnemosyne), the mother of the Muses, is the great dirt dump of humanity, the litter from which all letter is picked up. From the Muses comes museum, "This the way to the museyroom. Mind your hats goan in!" (8.10). "This way the museyroom. Mind your boots goan out" (10.22–23). In the museyroom we circle the square. Like hen men we can pluck up whatever chance offers us from memory, but to deliver it we must connect it to the logic of the postman.

Joyce took from Vico the claim that memory and imagination are the same. They are a coincidence of contraries. In the *New Science,* Vico says that memory has three different aspects: "memory [*memoria*], when it remembers things, imagination [*fantasia*], when it alters or simulates them, ingenuity [*ingegno*], when it encompasses them and puts them in proper guise and arrangement" (819, my trans.). Vico adds that this conception of memory is why the mother of the Muses was called Memory. These three aspects of memory explain the interrelationship of litter, letter, and literature. Memory as simply memory supplies litter. All that there is, ever was, and ever will come to be is in memory. As Jorge Luis Borges, in "The Immortal," the philosophical literary work with Vico as its basis, says, quoting Bacon: "Solomon saith: there is no new thing upon the earth. So that as Plato had an imagination, that all knowledge was but remembrance; so Solomon giveth his sentence, that all novelty is but oblivion."[38]

Memory is the great dirt dump of history from which, like the hen, we call things forth and resurrect them in the present to become the future. Letter, on which Joyce discourses in the early part of the *Wake*, is a particular narrative formed from the universal storehouse of memory. A letter is a personal narrative and, as we see in the *Wake*, not easily interpreted, but it brings what is in memory into an accessible form. A letter is a product of the imagination, a "fabulist's parable" (152.13) that we make from letters if we, following the instruction to Bruno Nowlan, take our tongues out of our inkpots.

From letter-writing comes literature. The particular narrative that takes the form of the letter drawn from the universal storehouse of memory must be formed as a universal fiction if it is to be realized as literature. Literature is produced by ingenuously extending the art of letters to a narrative, with an objective structure that aims at portrayal of the human condition itself. Literature gives us fictions of the human race that take us toward the philosophical concern with self-knowledge, and the philosophers must always go to school with the poets to attain a beginning point for this concern. Literature in turn is implicitly philosophical. In *Finnegans Wake* Joyce gets to literature through incorporating the universal elements of Bruno's and Vico's philosophy.

Shem and Shaun are rival twins, but they are also opposites within the same self and within human consciousness itself. They are a dialectic that coincides at the human level, unlike the opposites of Cusanus that can be reconciled only at the level of divine being. They are a twone that is wholly accessible to us. These opposites of Joycean psychology are justified by Vico's metaphysics of *corso* and *ricorso* that divide all history between them. *Corso* is the post that is reposted in the *ricorso*. The *ricorso* is an imitation or forgery of the original. Like a retrial or appeal, it reenacts what has already occurred in its own terms. It is not a duplicate of the *corso* because it is not identical with it. Thus *corso e ricorso* is not an identity of indiscernibles but a coincidence of contraries that is fully accessible to us.

Furthermore, within each there is a reconciliation of opposites in order to make each comprehensible. Opposites are not two separate entities that then must be reconciled. All beings are twones, such that the opposites that constitute them emerge from each other. Their reconciliation is the recognition of each that its opposite is the other that is also itself. The self-identity of each is itself turned back on itself. Their comprehensibility depends upon Vico's philological-philosophical method, what he calls the new critical art—*nuova arte critica*—through which philosophy undertakes to examine philology, understood as the analysis of the laws, languages, and customs of the nations at war and in peace.

These things particular to each nation are the certains (*i certi*) of its existence. The certains are part of the trues (*i veri*) of what is common to the nature of all the nations in the great city of the human race. The certains are the chance events, fixed by authority. The trues are the necessary principles, derived directly from reason. What is true of the whole of the human, the macrocosm, is true of each of its parts, its microcosms. Shem and Shaun are a way of seeing these interactions on a human level.

In Joyce's "inartistic portraits of himself" as Shem the Penman we "behond the shadow of a post!" (462.21–22)—Vico, the *custode* of knowledge, "the doublejoynted janitor" (27.02–3), who appears as a constant in the *Wake* as "the postface in that multimirror megaron of returningties, whirled without end to end" (582.19–21). In the pages of the *Wake* we are pursued by "the babbling pumpt of platinism" (164.10–11) through which we hear the thundering of the "postman's knock" (27.07). We are "posted ere penned" (232.17), as in that multimirror of the *Wake* litter becomes letter and letter becomes literature. To make his forgery of the new science Joyce, with his jokes, "promptly tossed himself in the vico" (417.05–6).

Since Joyce proclaimed he did not know if any of Bruno's or Vico's theories were true or not, he took from them what he found useful, but it is for his reader to know what the theories actually are from which he took—Joyce did.

Chapter 4

✦

Vico's Vita and the Producer (Mr. John Baptister Vickar)

Vico

John Bishop, in his chapter on the *New Science* and *Finnegans Wake* in *Joyce's Book of the Dark*, rightly rejects as superficial the received doctrine in Joycean criticism that the conception of cycles of history is what inspired Joyce in Vico's thought and what he primarily took from the *New Science*. As Bishop puts it: "The critical work on *Finnegans Wake* has failed to account fully for Joyce's passionate interest in Giambattista Vico's *New Science*. . . . most critics of the *Wake* have remained content to draw on a reading of Vico that had already become gelled, as early as 1950, into a received form destined to be passed on from study to study without much examination or modification."[1]

The idea that there are cycles in history is hardly what is new in the *New Science*. It was a constant view of the ancients, and Vico himself says he takes it from Herodotus and Varro. Bishop writes: "It is—and should be—hard to understand how the Vico portrayed in Joyce studies should have generated 'passionate interest' in Joyce long before he began the writing of *Ulysses*, let alone *Finnegans Wake* [as Ellmann reports]. . . . It is, moreover, difficult to understand how this received version of Vico could have caused Joyce to claim that *The New Science* strongly forced itself on his life or that Vico anticipated and yielded richer insights than Freud."[2] Joyce realized the greatness of Vico's thought and found a way to connect his imagination with Vico's. He did not simply employ Vico's thought as a grid to reinforce the base of his own vision.

Joyce is thinking of more than a grid when he merges his night with Vico's "night of thick darkness enveloping the earliest antiquity" in the *New Science* (331), which reflects Dante's "dark wood," the *selva oscura* of the first lines of the *Divine Comedy*, in which the "straight way was lost." Jorge Luis Borges says, in his late lectures on poetry: "When I speak of night, I am inevitably—and happily for us, I think—reminded of the last sentence of the first book in *Finnegans Wake*, wherein Joyce speaks of 'the rivering waters of, hitherandthithering waters of. Night!' This is an extreme example of an elaborate style. We feel that such a line could have been written only after centuries of literature. We feel that the line is an invention, a poem—a very complex web, as Stevenson would have had it. And yet I suspect there was a moment when the word 'night' was quite as impressive, was quite as strange, was quite as awe-striking as this beautiful winding sentence: 'rivering waters of, hitherandthithering waters of. Night!' "[3] Joyce reaches this night through those of Dante and Vico and, with little question, of Virgil before them.

My aim in this chapter and the one that follows is to help deliver the letter that Joyce wrote after reading and rereading Vico. Recall that, when Joyce was beginning to form the contents of *Finnegans Wake*, and, suffering with his failing eyesight, he desired to hear Vico's *Scienza nuova* again, he placed an advertisement in a Paris newspaper, hoping to find an Italian who would read it to him. My aim requires a more extensive and specific interpretation of Vico's philosophy than that in the received doctrine of Vico present in Joycean criticism—as a structural source for *Finnegans Wake*. Reading Joyce's work requires not only an understanding of the principles of the *New Science* but also an awareness of the presence of Vico's autobiography in it. Joyce drew on Vico's philosophical account of himself as well as his account of the common nature of the nations.

Joyce may intend a reference to Vico's autobiography when he connects autobiography to Shaun in his presentation of Shaun the Post in book 3 of the *Wake*: "Be trouz and wholetrouz! Otherwise, frank Shaun, we pursued, what would be the autobiography of your softbodied fumiform?" (413.29–31). To tell "the truth, the whole truth and nothing but the truth." Vico, the professor of Latin eloquence, author of a work on jurisprudence as large or larger than the *New Science*, *Il diritto universale* (*Universal Law*), claims that, unlike Descartes, he will not feign his account of his studies (as will be discussed below). He will tell the truth with candor: "frank Shaun." We must pursue his postman's story, told in his soft-bodied uniform.

Joyce refers to two other of Vico's early Latin works—*De antiquissima Italorum sapientia* (1710) and *De nostri temporis studiorum ratione* (1708/9). I have referred to the first of these earlier, in relation to the passage connecting Bruno's and Vico's Latin names: "*antiquissimam flaminum amborium Jordani et Jambapistae mentibus revolvamus sapientiam*" (287.23–25), and in the passage connecting Bruno and Vico to Quinet and Michelet: "The olold stoliolum! From quiqui quinet to michemiche chelet and a jambebatiste to a brulobrulo!" (117.10–12). In the *De antiquissima*, Vico derives his metaphysics by unearthing philosophical and theological meanings buried in the Latin language, which he claims had absorbed them from the Ionian philosophers and from the Etruscans, who were expert in sacred rites. These meanings, interred in Latin and spoken by Roman soldiers and farmers, are the most ancient wisdom of the Italians. Joyce derives such wisdom from the overlooked and obscure doctrines of the Italian texts of Bruno and Vico, unearthed for us by Quinet and Michelet.

As the Latin passage in the *De antiquissima* appears in the classbook section of the *Wake*, so does that on the *De nostri*, Vico's little book on education in which he seeks to balance the methods of the ancients against the moderns: "past Morningtop's necessity and Harington's invention, to the clarience of the childlight in the studiorium upsturts" (266.11–13). A few lines down is "After sound, light and heat," joined to the Vichian and Augustinian combination of "memory, will and understanding" (266.18–19). Vico's approach to education with the ancients is through the *ars topica*, which bases all learning on the cultivation of memory, and then proceeds to the *ars critica*, the logical training of will and understanding. Modern education, concerned only with scientific reasoning, focuses solely on the critical faculties and the training of the will to accord with them. But the children educated by Vico's method of studies will "newknow knowwell their Vico's road" (246.24–25).

Suggested in the image of the children beginning their day, the "upsturts" (who will rise and fall; German *Sturz*, fall) is Vico's theme of balancing the successes of the moderns against the accomplishments of the ancients: "necessity" and "invention" (principles of technology and science: necessity is the mother of invention—in this case, Harington's indoor privy or water closet,[4] the morning "necessary"), and "Sound, light and heat" (things the moderns have explained), against the ancients' expertise in memory and the education of the soul. In Vico's "studiorium" of "upsturts" the clarience of the childlight is awakened and becomes the basis for the education of the human spirit. The childhood of humans corresponds to the dawn of humanity that is repeated in the child and in each morning.

I intend to approach, not Joyce as the reader of Vico but Vico as the reader of Joyce. Jim the Penman has rewritten Vico's autobiography (1725, 1731) and the *Scienza nuova* (1725, 1730/44)—the only work for which Vico said he wished to be remembered—into a single text. Vico, in fact, wrote these two works at the same time. His autobiography is the history of himself and his *New Science* is the history of the human race. He employed the same principles in both cases. Like many scientists, he experimented with the principles of his science on himself first. In finding that this method of meditation worked for his own history, he also found that it worked for the history of humanity. It is a coincidence of contraries.

Vico's Fall

Recall that the first page of *Finnegans Wake* opens with a reference to Vico ("vicus"). But more than this, the first page of the *Wake* is a rewriting of the first page of Vico's autobiography, in which Vico, like Finnegan, falls headfirst from a ladder, fracturing his skull, and is not expected to live, but does. Vico is resurrected by God's grace in life. Finnegan dies but is awakened. On examining Vico, the surgeon predicted he would either die or grow up stolid (*stolido*). Vico does neither, but his personality is inverted from a "boy whose temperament was very lively and restless" to one of "a melancholy and acrid nature which necessarily belongs to ingenious and profound men, who through ingenuity flash like lightning in acuity, through reflection take no pleasure in witticism and falsity."[5]

Vico is reborn at the bottom of the first page of his autobiography, having fallen from the top of it. His fall was thunderous, incorporating within his mind the lightning that the giants respond to in order to be reborn as first humans of the gentile world. This temperament was combined with the classic melancholic temperament of the philosopher and of "Eve," Vico's mother. Vico falls at age seven, with the temperament of a child, and is reborn with the adult temperament of a philosopher.

Much has been said and can be said about Finnegan's fall on the first page of the *Wake*. The first page, as Joseph Campbell indicates in his own narrative of the *Wake*, contains much of the work itself.[6] Together with the last page, of which it is a part, it is the most important page in the book. Finnegan's fall is the fall of man from the Garden of Eden, inhabited by Eve and Adam, who appear in the first line of the *Wake*. Vico begins his autobiography by identifying his parents as representing two temperaments—his father having a cheerful disposition and his mother having a melancholy one. Vico tells us nothing more about his parents except they left a good name after them. Vico falls from the Garden of Eden that is the world of childhood. He is transformed from the childhood world of the senses to the world of acute mental activity and reflection.

In the ballad Tim Finnegan is a hod-carrier, represented by his "tipplin' way" because "with the love of liquor he was born."[7] Like one of Vico's *giganti*, he is a being who lives by his senses. His fall generates the first hundred-letter thunder word, the sound of divine providence that instills terror, for the first time, in Vico's *giganti*—and begins the resurrection of the human traits that they had lost when the sons of Noah giantized and began to wander the great forests of the earth after the universal flood, of which Vico speaks in the *New Science* (369–73).

In delivering the story of himself Vico is something of a penman. He fabricates his birth date, claiming that he was born in the year 1670 when actually he was born in 1668, and he always refers to himself by name or in the third person.[8] By claiming to have been born in 1670, Vico puts his end in his beginning—seventy years being the allotted or proper life span, according to both the Bible and Greek medicine—also incorporating his age, seven, at which his fall occurred, and incorporating the number sixteen, the age at which he claims to have won his first court case, brought against his father, the point at which he demonstrates his full powers of acuity. He concludes the 1731 continuation of his autobiography by likening himself to Socrates, saying he would be willing to undergo his fate if he could claim his fame. Socrates died at seventy, according to Plato.

The first page of the *Wake* brings Vico (*vicus*) back to life. He is alive (*vivus*) as his double, Finnegan, who revives from the whiskey spilled on him at his wake, to declare at the end of the ballad "do ye think I'm dead?" Vico's fall is Finnegan's fall. Finnegan is "*fine ancora*," "*fine* again," the end again. In Finnegan's name the *n* is doubled, as his name itself means something happening twice. It echoes Vico's line in his chapter on "Poetic Logic" in the *New Science,* in which he says human words were formed by interjections and from this principle concludes that the first word to be spoken by the inarticulate giants was an interjection imitating the thunderbolts of Jove. Vico states: "these interjections of Jove should give birth to one produced by the human voice: *pa!*; and that this should then be doubled: *pape!*" (448).

In Vico's and Finnegan's falls from the ladder we hear the sound of thunder, and the sound of thunder itself appears in Joyce's first thunder word: "The fall (bababadalgharaghtakamminarronnkonnbronntonner ronntuonnthunntrovarrhounawnskawntoohoohoordenenthurnuk!)." Vico's *pa* (*padre*) is taken up as *ba* (*babbo*, Italian "daddy"), and the whole hundred-letter word is composed of doubled letters and syllables and incorporates various words for thunder (e.g., French *tonnerre*, Italian *tuono*, Danish *tordenen*). Thunder as the first interjection is the Tower of Babel. It contains the beginnings of all languages that ever will be spoken.

The first word spoken by Jove or Jupiter Tonans and imitated as the first word spoken by the human voice is the complete speech at the basis of language itself. It is a naturalistic version of the Adamic language, spoken not by Adam but by the anonymous giants, founders of gentile humanity who became the fathers of the first families, from which the nations are born.

Once Vico appears as "vicus of recirculation," the Dublin of the old world of "Europe Minor" is doubled in the new world of "North Armorica." The doubled Dublin is born out of the forest cleared by "topsawyer," a recirculation of Vico's Hercules, who first made clearings in the great forest that covered the earth, after the universal flood, in which the first families lived and which later became cities. As Vico says, every nation had its Hercules, just as every nation had its Jove—although called by various names. Dublin, in Laurens County, Georgia, located on the Oconee River, was founded by a Dubliner, Peter Sawyer.

As mentioned earlier, Joyce came to know of this Dublin by asking Julien Levy to look up Dublins in America. Levy found there were three Dublins in the United States, and Joyce was anxious to know if any lay on a river.[9] Topsawyer is also associated with Mark Twain's Tom Sawyer of Hannibal, Missouri, on the Mississippi River, but a "topsawyer" is a worker at a sawpit who stands above the timber, opposite a bottom sawyer who stands below the timber in the pit. As Joseph Campbell observes, the topsawyer is Shaun and the bottom sawyer is Shem.[10] The two sawyers are opposites and doubles, reconciled in a single task. Once in their clearing, "Laurens County's gorgios" "went doublin their mumper [number] all the time." Any beginning recirculates the original beginning of the gentile nations, as Vico described it.

When Joyce places Vico's name in Latin in the first sentence of *Finnegans Wake* he provides the reader with the master key to the work. Vico declares to the reader that "the master key to this Science" is his discovery of the "poetic character" or "imaginative universal" (which will be discussed in the following chapter herein). By using Vico's Latin name, *vicus*, Joyce doubles Vico, since Latin is the original Italian. Vico says in his autobiography that he resolved early in his studies to master Latin to the level of his own language. *Vicus* further has the double meaning of "village" and "road." Thus when Vico's name is doubled the name with which it is doubled has a double meaning. The two doubles are a square which is circled by the roundheaded Vico.

The master key to *Finnegans Wake* is the act of doubling up. All is a "twone" (3.12). Everything can be doubled. Everyone is a double: "the humptyhillhead of humself" (3.20) and then Here Comes Everybody. In his autobiography Vico doubles himself in his fall, in which he is reborn at the beginning, and he doubles himself at the end when he presents himself as the Socrates of the new polis (*Neapolis*), the Italian Socrates of the third age of the *ricorso* that is the double of the Greek Socrates of the third age of the *corso*. Joyce has Vico as his double as Shem has Shaun in his rewriting of Vico's autobiography.

Vico's Fable

By referring to himself only by name or in the third person in his autobiography, Vico not only doubles himself; he also establishes the condition from which he can present the truth of himself as a fable. The first sentence of his autobiography accomplishes this condition: "Signor Giambattista Vico, he was born in Naples in the year 1670 of upright parents, who left behind them a very good reputation [*Il signor Giambattista Vico egli è nato in Napoli l'anno 1670 da onesti parenti, i quali lasciarono assai buona fama di sé*]."[11] Acting as his own biographer gives Vico the freedom to write as a historian and, in the manner of ancient historians, to give his birth date a rhetorical meaning regarding the number seven.[12]

The urtext for Vico's history of himself is Augustine's *Confessions*. In signing one of the sets of corrections and annotations to the *New Science*, Vico dates it as the eve of the feast day of Saint Augustine, who he says is "my particular protector [*il mio particulare protettore*]."[13] In his address to the Academy of Oziosi in 1737, in what was to be the last public presentation of his career, Vico closed his oration by calling upon Father Augustine, under whose protection, he reminded its members, the academy proceeds (there actually were other saints: Jerome, Thomas Aquinas, and Teresa) to formulate a prayer bringing Jove and Minerva together with "the omnipotent Your Father."[14] Vico's autobiography stands to the *New Science* as Augustine's *Confessions* stands to the *City of God*.

The term "autobiography" did not exist in Italian or any modern European language at the time of Vico. Thus his autobiography is titled *Vita di Giambattista Vico scritta da se medesimo*—*The Life of Giambattista Vico Written by Himself*.[15] In his 1731 continuation Vico says, reflecting on the first part, written from 1725 to 1728: "as may be seen, he wrote it as a philosopher, meditating the causes, natural and moral, and the occasions of fortune; why even from childhood he had felt an inclination for certain studies and an aversion from others; what opportunities and obstacles had advanced or retarded his progress."[16] Vico's autobiography, as its co-translator, Max Harold Fisch says, is "the first application of the genetic method by an original thinker to his own writings."[17] Vico's genetic account, however, like his ideal eternal history, is governed by providence, a point he makes clear in the conclusion to the above lines: "and lastly the effect of his own exertions in right directions, which were destined later to bear fruit in those reflections on which he built his final work, the *New Science*, which was to demonstrate that his intellectual life was bound to have been such as it was and not otherwise."[18]

Augustine's *Confessions* is a genetic account of the progress of his spirit from his childhood through his paganism to his conversion to Christianity and, in its final chapter, to his understanding of the meaning of Christianity. His *City of God* is the story of the emergence of Christian thought and culture from the virtuous pagans. Vico's *New Science* is the story of the emergence of the gentile nations, from the giants roaming the earth after the universal flood, to the age of humans.

Without saying so, Vico is imitating Augustine. It would be improper for him to compare his life as he tells it to the account Augustine gives of his. Vico is quite clear that his use of the genetic method is opposed to Descartes's pretended autobiographical account in the *Discourse on Method*. In the first pages of his autobiography, Vico says: "We shall not here feign what René Descartes craftily feigned as to the method of his studies simply in order to exalt his own philosophy and mathematics and degrade all the other studies included in divine and human erudition."[19]

Vico's reference is to Descartes's dismissal, from his standard of "right reasoning," of eloquence and history and all the fields of humane letters in which the ancients excelled and which, as mentioned above, Vico wished to balance with the sciences of the moderns.[20] Vico concludes: "Rather, with the candor [*ingenuità*] proper to a historian, we shall narrate plainly and step by step the entire series of Vico's studies, in order that the proper and natural causes of his particular development as a man of letters may be known."[21] Descartes presents himself as a figure in a tableau, making the discovery of the principles of his method while sitting at his *poêle* in a room in Ulm during a single day. Descartes presents his thought in *nature morte*. Vico presents his thought as *vera narratio*.

Augustine, in the *City of God*, praises the importance and perfection of the number seven. He says: "let it suffice to observe that the first odd integer is three, that four is the first even integer, and that the sum of these is seven. For this reason seven is often used to indicate universality."[22] He then cites Proverbs, the full line of which is: "For a righteous man falls seven times and rises again; but the wicked are overthrown by calamity" (24:16). Vico's autobiography can be comprehended in terms of seven falls and risings again. Each fall and each rising is always the end again. As Joyce says, "under his seven wrothschields lies one" (10.35).

Vico's first fall, a physical fall at age seven, from which he rises "by the Grace of God," is symbolic of the pattern of his whole life, which, as mentioned above, is governed by providence. His second fall is the loss in grammar school of a competition to be advanced to a higher grade, based on an unfair judgment by his teachers, who promoted a lesser student over him. His rise is to become an autodidact and remain so throughout his years of education. No one could teach Vico anything; he taught himself, the pinnacle of which was the program of reading he devised for himself while tutor in the Cilento to the children of the Rocca family.

His third fall is his return from the Cilento to Naples, after nine years, only to find himself a "stranger in his own land, and found the physics of Descartes at the height of its renown among the established men of letters."[23] Aristotle had become a laughingstock (*divenuta una favola*). The profundity of Greek wisdom and the grandeur of Roman oration were not to be found. But Vico counted himself fortunate to have been away and to have educated himself: "So for all these reasons Vico blessed his good fortune in having no teacher whose words he had sworn by, and he felt most grateful for those woods [of the region of the Cilento] in which, guided by his good genius, he had followed the main course of his studies untroubled by sectarian prejudice."[24] He had escaped exposure to the fashions of thought that change like the fashions of dress.

The fourth fall, matched only by the life-changing dimension of his first, was his loss of the concourse for the chair of civil law at the University of Naples, where he had earlier secured a lower position due to his classical learning. Like the unfair judgment of his abilities in the grammar school competition, the authorities gave the position to another, whose only book was later withdrawn from the press for plagiarism. Vico rose from this defeat by realizing the freedom he had gained—not to present his thought in Latin and in a manner acceptable to the academic world—for he could now write in Italian, like Galileo, and he could develop the idea of his new science of the nations from his earlier researches on the origin and nature of law.

Vico quickly completed what is known as the *First New Science* (1725), only to learn that the costs of its publication, which were to have been borne by Cardinal Corsini, to whom the volume was dedicated, were withdrawn because the cardinal had overspent funds on his recent travels. This was Vico's fifth fall. To arise from it he sold a family ring, the only item of monetary value in his possession, to publish the work himself.

The sixth fall was the appearance of a false book notice, of the publication of the *First New Science*, that appeared in the prestigious *Leipzig Acta Eruditorum*, mocking Vico as an author, saying he was an abbé of the Vico family, misrepresenting the nature of the work as a "large shapeless mass of his conjectures," and stating that "by the Italians themselves he is received more with tedium than with applause."[25] This false notice was sent to the *Acta* by several of Vico's university colleagues, led by his *gran tormentatore*, Nicola Capasso, a figure of no intellectual accomplishment. Vico arose from this attack by circulating his word-for-word response, known as the *Vici Vindiciae*, showing himself as a righteous and true scholar.

The seventh fall was the collapse of the offer to republish the *First New Science* in an expanded version in Venice, a center for scholarly publishing and a crossroads for contact between the intellectual worlds of northern and southern Europe. This new edition could secure for Vico the attention that he continually sought from the scholars of northern Europe. But after difficulties with the length of the work and with the Venetian printers, as he claims in his account in his autobiography, Vico withdrew the work to publish it in Naples.

His claim that he withdrew it because of the attitude of the Venetian printers is unconvincing. Evidence has emerged in just the past few years that there arose problems with ecclesiastical censorship.[26] They never fully materialized because Vico withdrew the work to Naples. But to publish the work it was necessary to rewrite the entire manuscript in a shorter version, which Vico accomplished in 106 days, between Christmas of 1729 and Easter of 1730, giving the book the form we have it in today, the version known as the *Second New Science*. Vico said that, of all his works, he wished for only the *New Science* to remain.

What might Joyce have seen in the figure of Vico when, in Trieste, he read Vico's autobiography, perhaps in the fifth volume (pub. 1911) of the new Laterza edition of Vico's works, while he was writing *A Portrait of the Artist as a Young Man*? He would have seen an Italian double of himself. Vico found himself a stranger in his own city, an expatriate in his own country. Vico left Naples for his tutoring position, and returned. Joyce left Dublin and found a tutoring position in Pola and then in Trieste. Joyce lived on Piazza Giambattista Vico and spoke passionately of Vico with some of his students. Like Vico, he knew Latin. Vico turned from Latin to write in his own language. Joyce sought, from *Dubliners* on, to write in his own language in a new way. Vico, the family man, struggled to provide for his family in a low-paid position. Joyce constantly struggled to make ends meet. Vico struggled to get his work published, as did Joyce. Joyce was a permanently lapsed Catholic. Vico proclaimed the glory of the Christian religion but developed views of man, history, and providence that are pagan in origin and intent.

Vico and Joyce were even physically similar. Vico had a skin and bones appearance, that, as Croce reports, caused people to apply to him the antique slur of "Mastro Tisicuzzo" (a reference to *tisico*, "tubercular," "having a tubercular appearance"). Joyce was thin—Lucie Léon-Noel—a fashion writer, the wife of Paul Léon, Joyce's friend and private secretary in Paris—described Joyce's appearance as that of a "thin man." The photographer Gisèle Freund said she was "struck by the paleness of his features."

Vico saw himself as living in his own city quite unknown, yet "born for the glory of his native city and therefore of Italy." Joyce, living in Trieste, saw himself in a similar way, otherwise he could not have carried on as the penman, seeing Vico as the roundheaded postman who had traveled this road before.

Vico's Resurrection

Finnegans Wake is the autobiography of everybody. As a single person, everybody is H. C. Earwicker. Vico is Earwicker and is sometimes Shaun, Earwicker's offspring. With Vico as protagonist, *Finnegans Wake* is a rewriting of Vico's *Vita*. Vico is the producer who makes his own truth. Implied in "the producer" is Vico's famous claim, put forth in his *De antiquissima*, that "the true is the made"—*verum esse ipsum factum*, or that "the true is convertible with the made"—*verum et factum convertuntur*.[27] Because human beings make the events that comprise history, they can in principle, if not fully in fact, make a knowledge of this history. The same holds for autobiography, as he who lives a life can make a knowledge of it—can formulate its truth. Shaun the postman can make and deliver this truth, but what he delivers will have been written by Shem the penman, and that will correspond to the fable of himself.

On October 25, 1725, after the publication of the first version of the *New Science*, Vico wrote to his Capuchin friend, Father Bernardo Giacco, that he felt himself to be "clothed as a new man," and that the work has filled him with a "heroic spirit" such that he does not fear death.[28] With the hands of Joyce the penman Vico is reclothed as a new man, as Earwicker. Pulled thus from the obscurity into which he and his work had fallen after their resurrection by Michelet, Vico is brought forth as a figure of the greatest work of modern literature.

By calling Vico the producer Joyce implies that it is Vico's thought that organizes the roles played out in the *theatrum mundi* of history, governed by the mother of the Muses as a theater of memory.[29] Vico's *New Science* is part of the great tradition of *teatro della memoria*[30] and the search for the *clavis universalis* of the complete encyclopedia.[31] *Finnegans Wake* stands astride these great traditions like the Colossus of Rhodes. Vico the producer is also the "Baptister," the thinker of rebirth that follows every birth. And Vico is the vicar, the custodian of divine knowledge—the agent of providentiality as present in history. As the custodian he attempts to appear as a "good catlick" (409.12) and is "the doublejoynted janitor" (27.02–3) who grasps history through the pairing of *corso* and *ricorso*. Vico's position in the Academy of Oziosi, to which, as mentioned above, he gave his last oration, was *custode*.

G. B. Vico is H. C. Earwicker. The initials of Earwicker can be derived from Vico's initials by cycling one letter forward in the alphabet, thus: G.→H. and B.→C. Vico's initials are renewed from Earwicker's by recoursing one letter backward. Vico is vic or "old vic" (62.06)→wick. "Wick" is a row of houses or a village, and is derived from *vicus*, Vico's Latin name. "W" is a double "v." The "v" is pronounced as "w" in classical Latin (*vicus*, pronounced "weekus"). Earwicker is Vico's name pronounced in English. We can hear Vico in "Earwicker."

Shaun is now "metandmorefussed" (513.31) into the sleeping Yawn in the third chapter of the third book of the *Wake*. The four old men who are trying to wake him and learn his identity are "cooched down a mamalujo by his cubical crib" (476.31–32). Like all of us, Yawn has a double: "I have something inside of me talking to myself" (522.26). Inside him is H. C. E., who in fact is Vico: "you may identify yourself with the him in you" (496.25–26). The *Wake* will bring this out with its "tales within tales" (522.05).

Shaun is Earwicker and since Earwicker is everybody he can take on a new name for any "time, place!" (546.24). But who is Earwicker really? "Whu's he?" (480.18). It is "Hunkalus Childared Easterheld. It's his lost chance" (480.20). To find out we must "talk very slowe!" (480.36). It is then revealed—Vico is H. C. E.'s middle name, the middle term of his syllogism:

> "—*Hail him heathen, heal him holystone*!
> *Courser, recourser, changechild,* . . . . ?
> *Eld as endall, earth* . . . . ?"[32]

Vico is the courser and recourser, the child of change. He is also the changeling, the child of circumstances, left by fairies in the cycles of history "—A cataleptic mithyphallic!" (481.04). Joyce continues: "—I have your tristich now; it recurs in three times the same differently"

(481.10–11). Each of the above three lines of this tristich or group of three lines of verse begins with one of the initials of H. C. E. Each recalls one of Vico's three ages of ideal eternal history. "—Hail him heathen" is the appearance of Jove the thunderer to the giants of Vico's first age of gods. The middle line is Vico himself, as if he were a heroic figure of the second age of heroes, and as a "heroic mind," as he portrays himself in the autobiography. *Eld* (Norwegian) is old age, the decline of society into the "barbarism of reflection" of Vico's third age of purely human thinking and things.

In the recourse, each age recurs "the same differently." All comes "from the human historic brute, Finnsen Faynean" (481.12–13). He is the father of "our family furbear" (132.32). We are all his offspring; he is the naturalistic Adam of the gentile nations. Thus "We speak of Gun, the farther. And in the locative. Bap! Bap!—Ouer Tad, Hellig Babbau, whom certayn orbits assertant re humeplace of Chivitas Ei" (481.19–21). "Babbau" is Italian "Babbo," "daddy," as mentioned earlier in connection to the first thunder word. Our "humeplace" is Saint Augustine's *De civitate Dei*. It is the "Ei" (German, egg). Vico is the father of our historical mentality, the founder of the philosophy of history that is the renewal of Father Augustine's "great city of the human race," the phrase that Vico applies to his conception of history. Vico is "dadaddy again" (496.28).

Earvico is the one who hears the thunder, that is, the one who hears the presence of providentiality in history as well as in his own telling of his own history. Vico has the ear for it, "for you cannot wake a silken nouse out of a hoarse oar" (154.09–10); "there's no-one Noel like him here to hear" (588.27–28); "the old hayheaded philosopher . . . old Earwicker" (47.01, 15); "the ear of Fionn Earwicker" (108.21–22); "Ear! Ear! Weakear!" (568.26); "Earwicker, that patternmind, that paradigmatic ear, receptoretentive as his if Dionysius" (70.35–36). Like "Dionysius's ear," the chamber in Dionysius's palace in Sicily through which he could overhear others, including his enemies, Vico can hear the murmurings in history that others cannot and comprehend their meanings in terms of his "patternmind." Vico can hear and see what others cannot. Vico is "earsighted" (143.09–10).

Earwicker is connected to earwig, the insect that was thought to crawl into ears. As an insect, an earwig has an extremely primitive appearance, something prehistoric in miniature. The word "earwig," in its archaic meaning, is a gossip and eavesdropper ("earwigging" is to circulate private talk). Gossip is language that circulates and often trades on the coincidence of events of which it speaks, of things also overheard. Joyce's Vichian ear hears everything and, through the use of all languages, circulates and recirculates what is heard and overheard. In his first axiom of the *New Science* Vico says: "In the long course that rumor [*fama*] has run from the beginning of the world, it has been the perennial source of all the exaggerated opinions which have hitherto been held concerning remote antiquities unknown to us" (121).

Joyce first introduces H. C. E. with a Vichian phrase: "a pleasant turn of the populace," and describes him as a universal individual: "which gave him as sense of those normative letters the nickname Here Comes Everybody. An imposing everybody he always indeed looked, constantly the same as and equal to himself and magnificently well worthy of any and all such universalisation" (32.17–21). Earwicker is an ironic version of a heroic imaginative universal (the nature of such universals is discussed in chapter 5 herein). In his fable of himself Vico presents himself in similar form. Anthony Burgess says: "The name 'Earwicker' does not seem to exist in real life. I have made a hobby to look for it in the telephone directories of all the towns I visit, but I have not yet found it, though *Earwaker* is often there—six times, as I remember, in the London directory."[33]

"Ear" is time as "wick" is place, "ever here and over there" (382.23). "Ear" is a play on "year" or "D'y'ear?" (Do you hear?). Year and place: whence and where (*unde et ubi*). Our sense of time physiologically is dependent on constant, small sound variations in the ear, not on sight. The visual experiences of time, the passages of day and night, the turning of the seasons, are secondary to the constant fluctuations of sound on the ear. Persons who become completely deaf (stone deaf, deaf as a post) can suffer difficulties with the sense of time passing because of the disappearance of sensitivity to these sound variations.

Vico has heard and reproduced the thunder, which Joyce remembers, imitates, and arranges into ten different forms so that we readers or listeners can hear, if we have ears to hear. "Loud, hear us!" (258.25). The thunders, being composed of thunder words from various languages, are mnemonic devices to allow us to contact the common mental language. As Joyce intended, the writing in *Finnegans Wake* is not just to be seen but to be read aloud. It is a "soundpicture" (570.14), "A halt for hearsake. A scene at sight" (279.09–280.01). When we put it in our ear we catch much more of its associations. "What can't be coded can be decorded if an ear aye sieze what no eye ere grieved for" (482.34–36).

Joyce often associates principles of the *New Science* with plays on Vico's name, or he simply plays on his name. There are plays just on "wick": "Eelwick" (134.16), "wicker" (108.23), "Stick wicks in your earshells" (435.19–20), "wick's ears pricked up" (83.06), "the wickser in his ear"

(311.11). There are plays on "vic": "the old vic" (62.06) (also the London theater), "Old Vickers" (330.13), "victimisedly victorihoarse" (472.20), "because avicuum's not there at all" (473.06–7), "V.I.C.5.6" (495.31) (the *New Science* has five books and the *corso* and *ricorso* have a total of six ages, and within an age Vico also speaks of six phases; see axiom 66); "six vics odd" (82.27), "*victis poenis hesternis*" (596.06–7) (yesterday's punishments having been overcome, there is a return), "the ubideintia of the savium is our ervics fenicitas" (610.07–8) (Dublin's motto: "Obedientia civium urbis felicitas"—Citizen's Obedience Is City's Happiness).

Vico is both vicar and viker: "watchouse in Vicar Lane" (84.18–19), "Vikens" (331.20), "our friend vikelegal" (131.21–22), "Viker Eagle" (622.08) (the eagle being the sign of Jove, Vico's *Jupiter Tonans*), and vicar in Middle English, "viker," which is from Late Latin *vicarius*, from *vicis* "change," "turn," which is the Latin source for "week" (*vicus*, "weekus"), "Vikloefells" (626.18), "Vikloe vich he lofed" (375.33), "murrmurr of all the mackavicks" (101.33), "Sheem avick" (188.05), "she vicking well knowed them all heartswise and fourwords" (279.F20–21), "*The victar*" (349.25), "the aboleshqvick" (302.18), "Shattamovick?" (354.01–2), "from livicking on pidgins'" (463.28), "*he confesses to all his tellavicious nieces*" (349.28), "the vicar's joy" (596.20), "me and my Riley in the Vickar's bed!" (495.17–18) ("The Ballad of Persse O'Reilly" [44.24–47.29], *perce-oreille*, French "earwig," Earwicker), "vicariously known as Toucher 'Thom' who is. I suggest Finoglam as his habitat" (506.28–29).

Viker is similar to Viking, as Earwicker was one of the Scandinavian invaders of Dublin. Vico is both the vicar and the Viking, the stability of the divine order in history and the instability of the political order. Vico via Earwicker also has associations with authority in the sense of viceroy, the king's representative, "Vikeroy" (100.05). H. C. Earwicker is spoken of "throughout his excellency long vicefreegal existence" (33.30–31); "his viceregal booth" (32.36), "viceking's graab" (18.13); "vicemversem" (384.27); "vicereversing" (227.19); "viceuvious" (570.05–6); "he was made vicewise" (286.29). The truth of Vico's authority (*auctoritas*) is made in history and can convert to its opposite, "Viceversounding" (355.10).

There is "Dr. Tipple's Vi-Cocoa" (26.30–31) taken over from "Dr. Tibble's Vi-cocoa" in *Ulysses* (Vico is a doctor of Triple, Doctor Threes; here also is one of Vico's first interpreters, Vincenzo Cuoco); "*Jambaptistae*" (287.24) and "as Jambudvispa Vipra foresaw of him" (596.29–30) (from Sanskrit *vipra*, "wise"); "promptly tossed himself in the vico" (417.05–6); "Noo Soch Wilds and from Vico" (497.13); "disguised as a vincentian" (38.26); "some navico, navvies" (179.19); and "Nearapoblican" (172.23) (the Neapolitan).

There are plays on the Vico road: "their Vico's road" (246.25), "Vicarage Road?" (291.18), "The Vico road goes round and round to meet where terms begin" (452.21–22), "Vicus Veneris" (551.34), and "the viability of vicinals if invisible is invincible" (81.01) ("vicinals," derived from *vicinus*, "neighboring"; vicinal roads as distinguished from highways). Roads are connected to circles: "closed his vicious circle, snap. Jams jarred" (98.19) ("James jarred" = James Joyce); the vicious circle was closed because it was "scrapheaped by the Maker" (98.17) (that is, by Providence), "moves in vicous cicles yet remews the same" (134.16–17). "We drames our dreams till Bappy returns. And Sein annews" (277.17–18). "Now, to be on anew" (143.03).

Enough has been said and quoted to demonstrate the full presence Vico has as a protagonist in *Finnegans Wake*. One turns a page, and there is Vico again in some new form, to be heard and seen in yet another way, in another guise. Vico the human figure is resurrected by Joyce, along with the principles of his new science. We encounter in John Baptister Vickar what Stephen went forth to encounter at the end of *A Portrait*. We encounter from the "old father, old artificer" "the producer" for the "millionth time," the "uncreated conscience" of our race. Joyce resurrects many figures in the *Wake* and Vico is one of them—a key figure.

Chapter 5

✦

Vico's Science and the Millwheeling Vicociclometer

The Vico Philosophy

Those interpretations of *Finnegans Wake* in the Joycean critical literature that give any attention to Vico's *New Science* focus almost entirely on Vico's conception of history as *corso* and *ricorso*. In the preceding chapter I agreed with Bishop, that the idea that events repeat themselves in history can hardly account for Joyce's attachment to Vico. Taken as such, as Isaiah Berlin once remarked, *corso* and *ricorso* is Vico's least original idea. No Joycean commentator has inquired into exactly what Vico's principle of *corso* and *ricorso*, what Vico calls "ideal eternal history" (*storia ideale eterna*) entails. Joyce refers to it in the classbook section as "PROBAPOSSIBLE PROLEGOMENA TO IDEAREAL HISTORY" (262.R1), one of a list of principles that take the reader through the main claims of the *New Science*. What does Vico mean by this term, "ideal eternal history"? In what way does his new science depend upon it as one of its central tenets?

Vico takes the title of the *Scienza nuova* from Galileo's famous *Dialoghi delle nuove scienze* and, to some extent, from Bacon's *Novum Organum*. Galileo had achieved a knowledge of the nature of motion that was the foundation of the modern science of nature. Bacon had replaced the Aristotelian *Organon*, with its focus on the deductive structure of the syllogism, with a logic of the inductive investigation of nature. In his autobiography, Vico designates Bacon as one of his four authors whom he will keep before him at all times. The other modern author is Grotius; the two ancients are Plato and Tacitus. Vico's square is composed of two "heretics" (Protestants) and two pagans. Plato, Vico says, shows man as he should be, and Tacitus, the historian, shows man as he is. Bacon's four idols correspond to the first four axioms of the *New Science*,[1] and Vico called Grotius the first prince of natural law. Vico admires Grotius, but he also disagrees with him.

Galileo and Newton have given us a new science of the motions of nature. Is it possible to discover a new science of the motions in the human world of nations? This is Vico's question. His further question, and one that lies within the first, is: what has kept us from discovering such a science already? Vico in the *New Science* wishes to accomplish for the human world what the founders of modern science have accomplished for the natural world. His guiding principle of method is that stated in axiom 106: "Doctrines must take their beginning from that of the matters of which they treat" (314).

The *New Science*, like Vico's autobiography, employs the genetic method. It requires a form of thought that can take us back to the form of the first thought of humanity and then course us forward from this to today. Vico's axiom 106 must be joined to axiom 66 (to which, as mentioned earlier, Beckett called our attention): "Men first feel necessity, then look for utility, next attend to comfort, still later amuse themselves with pleasure, thence grow dissolute in luxury, and finally go mad and waste their substance" (241). "History," as Stephen says in *Ulysses*, "is a nightmare from which I am trying to awake." The third age of Vico's ideal eternal history is one of luxury of living conditions coupled with rational madness brought on by the barbarism of reflection of modernity (which will be discussed later in this chapter).

Vico realized that the impediment to a successful science of the world of the nations was the commitment of the seventeenth-century natural-law theorists to the doctrine that human society originates through a social contract, or what Hobbes calls a covenant. Grotius, Pufendorf, and Selden, as well as Hobbes, held that society originates by an agreement to live under government in order to terminate an original, lawless state of human existence, in which the stronger held power by force over the weaker. Such a contract occurs due to the realization that, while it is good to do wrong, it is not good to be wronged. Power is transferred from the stronger few into the artificial man of the state. This terminates the Hobbesian war of all against all and an existence in which life is "solitary, poore, nasty, brutish, and short."

Vico's narrative of the origin of society in the *New Science* is opposed to this one that sees society as established by a collective act of self-reflection, whether its doctrine is held as having been an event that actually took place in the history of humanity or simply asserts it as a reasonable assumption to account for the origin of society. Vico retells the biblical story of the universal flood to account for the rise of the gentile nations and the presence of the ancient Hebrews. Following the flood, the earth is transformed into great trackless forests, in which the offspring of the sons of Noah—Ham, Japheth, and Shem—wander, growing in bodily size to that of giants and procreating without any family structure or institutions for the rearing of children. Humanity lives like beasts (*bestioni*), having lost the customs of religion, marriage, and burial of Hebrew culture before the flood (301).

As this wandering occurred, the earth dried out over two centuries. The race of Ham, the Hamites, wandered through southern Asia, Egypt, and the rest of Africa; that of Japheth, the Japhetites, wandered through northern Asia or Scythia and through Europe, but that of Shem, the Semites, remained in middle Asia, and a portion of them preserved the customs, education, and religion of their ancestors. This portion also remained of natural human stature. They became the ancient Hebrews, and maintained themselves in isolation from the Hamites and Japhetites, who became the race of giants from whence came the gentile nations (369).

These giants lived in a world of both physical and mental wandering, in which every facial expression was a new face, a world of immediacy without language. They experienced fear only in the sense of the motivation to self-preservation in the face of immediate danger from wild beasts or other giants. Once the earth was sufficiently dry, however, they suddenly encountered a new phenomenon—the sky, which they thought no higher than the treetops, lit up with flashes of thunderous lightning. This new phenomenon brought forth in them a fear of a different kind; it was not *paura* but great *timore* or *spavento*—terror. It was not the fear of an imminent danger but a fear coursing throughout their being.

To be human is to be the one animal that takes its existence as a problem: to wonder what it is to be human. The *spavento* of the *giganti* is the first glimmering of the problem, and by it these protohumans began to return to the human world from which their ancestors had descended. At the same time they experienced an absolute other: the sky divides from the earth as an alter-body. It is the first act of providence. They recovered the rudimentary power of human memory, which is the ability to have one sensation in the stream of sensations become the fixed meaning of the other moments of sensation. For those of the giants who responded to the terror of the lightning and thunder in this way, they imitated the sound of thunder in their voices and speech—the first word was the outcry of *Jove*. Instead of each instance of thunder being a unique event, these instances are all the appearance of the single sensation of Jove. As they began to think and recover their human minds they began physically to reduce to normal stature.

This most fundamental passion of fear gives rise, in those giants that can experience it, to a second passion—shame or modesty, *pudore*. Jove looks down on them and they go into caves to procreate out of Jove's sight, to form marriage and families. These first fathers formed religion by taking the auspices of Jove's action in the sky, which satisfies a third new passion, their curiosity, causing them to notice what is beyond themselves. They reinstitute the burial of the dead, which establishes lineage and property and takes them farther from their original brute existence. As Joyce says in *Ulysses*, "Only man buries." Not all of the giants are capable of transforming the terror of thunder into Jove and recovering the principles of humanity. Those giants remain feral and continue to wander the forests outside the clearings made as the places of the first families. They then seek the protection of the fathers of the first families, and become *famuli*, indenturing themselves to each paterfamilias.

From the clearings come cities and the order of society, based on the figures of the heroes who embody the virtues necessary for the development of the human sense of morality. The *famuli* are replaced by the *socii*, who become the attendants of the heroes and their dependents. From the cities are born nations, for as the name implies, a nation is a birth, *nascita*, *nascere*, "to be born." The nations are not nation-states but *gens*, peoples, groups of families held together by common customs, laws, and languages—a *sensus communis*—a communal sense. As the nations develop, written law replaces custom, the heroic language of emblems is replaced by articulate alphabetic language, and thought proceeds through abstract universals instead of imaginative images.

A nation, like a human organism, is born, and it rises, matures, declines, and falls in a cycle of mortality. Within the life of a nation there is a dialectic of social classes in which the nobles, the inheritors of the status of the fathers of the first families, extend their power forcefully over the plebeians, the inheritors of the status of the *famuli*, and the plebeians respond and collectively demand and obtain rights. The movement is from aristocracy, the rule of the best, to democracy, the rule of the hoi polloi. Finally the social order becomes a barbarism of rights upon rights upon rights until any given nation becomes rotten in this civil disease and men go mad and waste their substance. If they are not overrun from without by a stronger nation or a ruler does not arise among them, providence brings the nation to an end and its citizens are brought back to a life lived in terms of the necessities of existence, correspondent to that of the origins of the nation.

Vico's narrative of the origin of the nations puts forth his philosophy as an alternative to that of the natural-law theorists. To establish his work as a new science, Vico requires a universal principle upon which the narrative is based. Science requires universality. Vico must advance an understanding of something that is true of all nations; as his full title of the *New Science* indicates, his new science is one "concerning the common nature of the nations" (*d'intorno alla comune natura delle nazioni*) (1730/44). Vico finds what is needed in the claim of the first book of *The Digest of Justinian* regarding the origin of law: that there is a law of nations or *ius gentium* "which all human peoples observe."[2] *Ius gentium* is the concept of actual natural law, that there is a part of every system of law that is held in common with all other systems of law. *Ius gentium* is distinct from *ius civile* or positive law, that body of law distinctive to a particular nation or people. It is also distinct from *ius naturale* in the sense of a rational ideal that is conceived as a standard of right existing above and apart from any nation's system of law to which its system stands in relation—what Vico calls the natural law of the philosophers.[3]

Ius gentium is the common nature of the nations, but as it appears in the *Digest* it is a static principle of unity among nations. Vico regards Roman law as the perfect and complete system of civil wisdom. Thus what the Greeks sought in terms of *philosophia*, the Romans formulated as *iurisprudentia*. There are no rights to be claimed apart from those stated explicitly in Roman law: there is a right, if and only if the right is so stated. As a professor of Latin eloquence, Vico taught the principles of rhetoric centered in forensic rhetoric, the basis for interpreting law and speaking in the law courts. Vico taught this as his subject from his own textbook, his *Institutiones Oratoriae*, throughout his long career.

The title of the first version of his *New Science* emphasizes that it contains "the principles of another system of the natural law of the peoples" (*i principi di altro sistema del diritto naturale delle genti*). Vico accomplishes this system by transforming the *ius gentium* as the natural law of the nations into the doctrine of "ideal eternal history." He formulates the *ius gentium* as the dynamic principle of his historical narrative such that the common nature of the nations is that they all develop through a *corso* and *ricorso* of three ages—an age of gods, of heroes, and of humans.

To prove that this historical formulation of the *ius gentium* is universal and so to complete his science, Vico requires a new method, appropriate to the investigation of human phenomena. Like the method of the modern sciences of nature, it will be both empirical and logical in the sense of producing explanations from a small set of axioms and postulates that will connect with the facts or "certains" of history. Vico's method is both logical and rhetorical, based on what he terms a "new critical art" (*l'arte nuova critica*). This art or method is formed by joining philology with philosophy. By philology Vico means the study and analysis of the customs, laws, deeds, and languages of the life of the nations, at war and in peace.

The philologists have failed by half because their analyses are not connected to any universal principles. Their thought is simply descriptive, historical. The philosophers have failed by half in that they have produced accounts of the universal principles of human nature without grounding them in the details of human history. They have shown how human nature should be conceived apart from showing how such conceptions connect with how human beings actually are. Vico's method in the *New Science* is also rhetorical in that he employs *ars topica* to generate his narrative and combines this with *ars critica* to evaluate it and prove it by ordering it according to his axioms and postulates, using Bacon's method of "think and see" (*cogitare videre*) (359).

Vico's *New Science* is a complete speech that interrelates the three worlds—natural, human, and divine (42). In it he must distinguish nature from human nature on one side and from divine nature on the other. Human nature is the middle term of the great syllogism of the world. It is wisdom as defined by Cicero to be a knowledge of things divine and human and the causes of each.

The Master Key

Finnegans Wake is Vico's complete speech renewed, guided by the claim that caught Joyce's imagination, that "imagination is memory" (*la memoria è la stessa che le fantasia*). As pointed out earlier, the *New Science* is a great theater of memory, "our worldstage's practical jokepiece" (33.02–3), a great museum or "museyroom," as is *Finnegans Wake*. We enter both texts and our memory allows us to imagine everything. Vico's science is a science of imagination in this sense, as is its renewed version in Joyce's work, in which it "remews the same" (134.17). It is "the seim anew. Ordovico or viricordo [Italian *vi ricordo*, I remember you]." And, the order (Italian *ordine*) will be that of the Muses. "Anna was, Livia is, Plurabelle's to be," whose mother is Memory (ALP) (215.23–24).

In Joycean criticism it has been pointed out how much Joyce is influenced by Vico's conception of language as the basis of human consciousness and his use of etymology to support his claims. These observations are correct, but what is at the base of them? What is at the base of Vico's view of language and imagination that Joyce perceived, and in which he found the base of his own use of language?

In a rare declaration, perhaps the only one of its kind in the history of philosophy, Vico informs his reader of the master key to his *New Science*. He states: "We find that the principles of these origins both of languages and letters lies in the fact that the first gentile peoples, by a demonstrated necessity of nature, were poets who spoke in poetic characters. This discovery, which is the master key of this Science, has cost us the persistent research of almost all of our literary life" (34). These poetic characters (*carattere poetici*), he says, are certain "imaginative genera" (*generi fantastici*) which he also in various places calls "imaginative universals" (*universali fantastici*). At the beginning of the marginal notes in the classbook section of the *Wake*, summarizing the principal terminology of the *New Science*, is: "IMAGINABLE ITINERARY THROUGH THE PARTICULAR UNIVERSAL" (260.R).

Vico adds to the passage quoted above the point that he makes several times in the *New Science*, that because of "our civilized natures we cannot at all imagine and can understand only by great toil the poetic nature of these first men" (34). Vico describes for us the logic of these imaginative or particular universals, but as he asserts, he cannot actually take us inside the mentality that thinks and lives solely in terms of them. Joyce, however, does not leave this issue where Vico leaves it. From the first page of *Finnegans Wake* he takes the reader directly into the language of particular universals, the language of the origin of all humanity. From the standpoint of his science Vico cannot do this. But Joyce the penman can. Vico can only deliver the information about the original existence of such universals and explain what they are. Joyce explains nothing and delivers no information on the nature of language. Instead he takes us directly into the night world, the only world in which modern man can reach them, the world of the speech of imaginative universals, the original speech in which things themselves are spoken out. The reason *Finnegans Wake* is so difficult to read is because it is the speech of imaginative universals.

If we can imagine Vico's first humans—after they have developed the power of "mute" speech and perhaps even the later heroic or "emblematic" speech—being able to read or to hear read aloud his "tales within tales," they would without difficulty attain its comprehension and enjoyment. It would be *la sapienza poetica che parla*, poetic wisdom speaking, the original eloquence. They would be as puzzled as to why we could not grasp it as we are puzzled as to why they could.

What is an imaginative universal? It is the figure of a single individual, actual or mythical, univocally predicated of a group or series of other individuals that are held to be it. The nature of imaginative universals was briefly discussed in relation to Plato's quarrel with the poets, but we may pursue it further here. A prime example Vico gives in his axioms in the

New Science concerning imaginative universals is the figure of Godfrey in Torquato Tasso's poem *Jerusalem Delivered*.[4] Vico says: "poetic truth is metaphysical truth, and physical truth which is not in conformity with it should be considered false. Thence springs this important consideration in poetic theory: the true war chief, for example, is the Godfrey that Torquato Tasso imagines; and all the chiefs who do not conform throughout to Godfrey are not true chiefs of war" (205).

As an imaginative universal Godfrey is *not* a figure of a true war chief that functions as an archetypal individual to which other individuals are likened. Rather, for the mythopoetic mentality, these other individuals literally *are* Godfrey, and in addition, Godfrey is Godfrey. The relationship is not one of *similarity* but *identity*. The predication involved is universal in the same sense that the class term "war chief" as a concept in modern, rational mentality can be literally predicated of this, that, and the next individual war chief. To the modern mind there is nothing strange about universally predicating a common property of various individuals who are all members of the same class. So, to the mythopoetic mind there is nothing strange about apprehending these individuals as all equally Godfrey. They all equally share his identity. They are Godfrey and Godfrey is them, as well as being Godfrey.

A way to comprehend this in modern ethnological terms is to understand that the members of the Bear Clan do not think of themselves as *like* bears but that they literally are bears along with the bears. Linguistic identity comes before similarity in the development of consciousness and is presupposed by it. This is a doctrine of metaphor that is metaphysical in nature. It brings a thing into existence for the mind and precedes the Aristotelian doctrine of metaphor, which is epistemological in nature, being a way of combining two things already with their own identities, that is, asserting the name of one thing for another to which a similarity is alleged.

Joyce's language of imaginative universals is continually bringing new things into existence that we can allow ourselves to hear and see and to which we can react. When we interpret them intellectually, however, we then turn them into epistemological similarities or ironies. They can be ironies because irony, like metaphor, puts the name of one thing in the place of another, but in irony the purpose is to create a meaning through its opposite. A pun requires a sense of irony that is not open to the mythopoetic mind. The master key to *Finnegans Wake* is the pun, which always unsettles any fixed meaning that is reached by rationality. Joyce's irony is Socratic irony; it is done to achieve a meaning not available in the literal sense of words.

The imaginative or particular universal is the source of doubling. In the example of Godfrey the war chief, the other war chiefs are doubles of Godfrey. They are the same and yet separate. They are doubles of Godfrey and of themselves. Vico's *New Science* of poetic characters is an "IMAGINABLE ITINERARY" because we can think and react both metaphorically and ironically. Vico says that the trope of metaphor is the first of the four classic tropes and the fourth trope is irony. The mind of poetic wisdom of mythmaking can only state the truth, for myth is *vera narratio*. Irony arrives with the philosophers and reflective thought, in the third age of ideal eternal history. The intervening tropes are metonymy and synecdoche, ways of consciously forming metaphors. Our itinerary is open only to the imagination, for we cannot reason our way back to the mentality of the protohumans who found the gentile nations, nor can we reason our way back to our child-minds, when we first experienced the world. Only *Finnegans Wake* can take us there.

In sleep, reason goes to sleep, to awaken only when we awake. Sleep provides the natural condition for the imagination, a condition of human existence open to everyone, not just to those who have ability in poetic imagination. The dream, a constant of human life, is the first province of imagination. Vico's term for imagination is *fantasia* (literally, fantasy), but it is best understand as the "making" imagination. The giants make their world through *fantasia*; they bring the things of their world into existence by the power of *fantasia* to form images. *Fantasia* can be distinguished from *immaginazione* or the power to collect sensations into an image that can be then formed by reason into a concept. *Immaginazione* mediates between sensation and thought. *Fantasia* turns our feelings and passions or sensations of the world into a way of thinking. We feel the world in order to think it. What Vico discovers is that myth is a form of thought.

If we imagine Vico as reader of Joyce, he would immediately see that Joyce has given us, as much as it can be given to us, the original thought-form of humanity. What Vico in his science despaired of reaching, Joyce puts right into our ear. The Earwicker that is our constant double is always lying below the surface in the common mental language that echoes unrecognized in our own rationally, commonsensically induced speech. Vico says that the law by which we are first wholly humanized is originally a serious or severe but true poem (*severo e vero*). Joyce's *Wake* is a serious or severe joke, a poetic joke, a joke based on the principles of poetic characters as understood by Vico. Reading *Finnegans Wake* we learn not to take ourselves seriously, because in our earsighted reading we realize that we are only the offspring of our great "family furbear."

The Barbarism of Reflection

The first of the two most memorable and most quoted passages in the *New Science*, one that Bishop makes a great deal of, is this:

> But in the night of thick darkness enveloping the earliest antiquity, so remote from ourselves, there shines the eternal and never failing light of a truth beyond all question: that the world of civil society has certainly been made by men, and that its principles are therefore to be found within the modifications of our own human mind. Whoever reflects on this cannot but marvel that the philosophers should have bent all their energies to the study of the world of nature, which, since God made it, He alone knows; and that they should have neglected the study of the world of nations, or civil world, which, since men had made it, men could come to know (331).

The truth beyond all question is that we can have a knowledge of ourselves because we are the cause of this knowledge, although we are not the cause of ourselves. We are the product of providence. Vico's science is a response to the inscription on the *pronaos* of the Temple of Apollo at Delphi—*gnothi seauton*—that was advocated by both Socrates and Solon. Vico's science is the science of self-knowledge. Of the natural world we cannot have *scientia* but only *conscientia* (consciousness or conscience). Our understanding of nature is a matter of "witnessing conscience," of truly apprehending or observing the motions of nature to which scientific experiment is the key, since in experiment we come as close as is possible to making the things or events investigated. God as maker of the natural world can know by making and make by knowing. We can enact this conversion of the true and the made only in relation to ourselves, our motions in history. We cannot enact it in relation to the natural world. The night of thick darkness (*densa notte di tenebre*) is an echo, as mentioned earlier, of Dante's *selva oscura* that marks the beginning of the *Divine Comedy*.

Vico's "night of thick darkness" passage is matched by one of the two most memorable passages in *Finnegans Wake*—the subject of Borges's comment quoted earlier—the conclusion to the soliloquy on Anna Livia Plurabelle:

> Can't hear with the waters of. The chittering waters of. Flittering bats, fieldmice bawk talk. Ho! Are you not gone ahome? What Thom Malone? Can't hear with bawk of bats, all thim liffeying waters of.

> Ho, talk save us! My foos won't moos. I feel as old as yonder elm. A tale told of Shaun or Shem? All Livia's daughtersons. Dark hawks hear us. Night! Night! My ho head halls. I feel as heavy as yonder stone. Tell me of John or Shaun? Who were Shem and Shaun the living sons or daughters of? Night now! Tell me, tell me, tell me, elm! Night night![5] Telmetale of stem or stone. Beside the rivering waters of, hitherandthithering waters of. Night! (215–16)

It is part of the only passage which we can hear Joyce recite, in the only recording he made.

"Talk save us!" Serve us. We only have words with which to go into that night in which we can hardly hear, "Can't hear with the waters of." As we pass into our world of night, of sleep, we can hear the river Styx, and we wish to remember what was the "tale told of Shaun or Shem," the two opposites of our self, the coincidence of our contraries. The night, like ALP, the mother of the Muses of the knowledge of what was, is, and is to be, Memory, takes us to the end of the book of the night. "Far calls. Coming, far! End here. Us then. Finn, again! Take. Bussoftlhee, mememormee!" (628.13–14). "Adieu, adieu, Hamlet. Remember me" (said by his father's ghost to Hamlet; far = father in Danish). Hamlet replies, "Remember thee? Ay, thou poor ghost, while memory holds a seat in this distracted globe. Remember thee? Yea, from the table of my memory" (1.5.91, 95–98). Sleep will release the contents of the table of memory that will circulate for us by our imagination, unrestricted by the light of reason.

Why should we read the *New Science* or *Finnegans Wake*? We should read them because we live among barbarians. It is now the third age of Vico's *ricorso*, the age of rational madness, the point at which "men go mad and waste their substance," or to put it in a Vichian sentence of Rousseau's: "Finally, they chased the gods out in order to live in the temples themselves." Joyce and Vico can say with Ovid in *Tristia*, whose line is Rousseau's epigraph: "Here I am the barbarian because no one understands me."[6]

In the interpretation of the letter in book 1 of the *Wake* we find a reference to the second most memorable passage from the *New Science*: "the use of the homeborn shillelagh as an aid to calligraphy shows a distinct advance from savagery to barbarism" (114.12–13). Vico says:

> But if the peoples are rotting in that ultimate civil disease and cannot agree on a monarch from within, and are not conquered and preserved by better nations from without, then providence for their

> extreme ill has its extreme remedy at hand. . . . through long centuries of barbarism, rust will consume the misbegotten subtleties of malicious wits that have turned them into beasts made more inhuman by the barbarism of reflection than the first men had been made by the barbarism of sense. For the latter displayed a generous savagery, against which one could defend oneself or take flight or be on one's guard; but the former, with a base savagery, under soft words and embraces, plots against the life and fortune of friends and intimates. (1106)

This passage too echoes Dante, specifically the lowest level of the Inferno, where lie the sins of the *lonza*, the treacheries against guests and hosts, against family and relatives. These are the sins that employ malicious wit, that erode the very fabric of society, the bonds of trust that hold the customs, obligations, and friendships upon which society ultimately rests.

The barbarism of sense (*barbarie del senso*) is one of the uncontrolled passions of the bodily existence of the first humans. It is a savagery of the senses, but an honest and direct savagery of sensuous existence. The barbarism of reflection (*barbarie della riflessione*) is that of the civil disease of luxury of the third age, in which written law, subject to mean whatever it can be interpreted to mean, has replaced custom and heroic virtue and in which abstract reasoning and witty speech have replaced the power of the imagination to form images of the human.

There is no defense against the corruption of the mind in which it can use reason as an instrument of power. There is no end to argument and counter-argument and suspicion and counter-suspicion. At this stage of civil disease, how can we renew our humanity? How can we recover self-knowledge, the subject of the heroic mind of Socrates? In the *ricorso* we have lost the origin, and the solution is to recover the sense of the origin. As Joyce indicates in the *Wake,* we can know who we are only if we know from where and whence "UNDE ET UBI" (260R) we come. We must reaffirm memory, which takes us: "A way a lone a last a loved a long the riverrun, past Eve and Adam's, from swerve of shore to bend of bay, brings us by a commodious vicus of recirculation back to Howth Castle and Environs."[7] Back to H. C. E.

This, I think, is part of the other most memorable passage in *Finnegans Wake*, for everybody knows that it begins with the last half of a sentence, and that poses the question of exactly what is the first sentence of the *Wake*. The square of Eve and Adam's and Howth Castle and Environs is circled from the start. The circle is accomplished by the commodious vicus of recirculation. Here stands Vico, at the beginning and end of the book of doublends jined. We cannot do without him, for he is the one who delivers us the origin. Vico shows us the course to find the answer to "where in the waste is the wisdom?" (114.20). We can save ourselves with words if we can hear how they arise from the common mental language, and for this we will require "two thinks at a time." We will require "doublecressing twofold thruths and devising tingling tailwords too" (288.03–4) in order to keep ourselves from going rationally mad by abandoning memory and living only in the daylight of the conceptually ordered present. We must reveal history not as a single causal order of events but as a circle of "cocoincidences" (597.01). This is our new sense of providential order.

Providentiality

To Vico's three ages of ideal eternal history—gods, heroes, and humans—Joyce adds a fourth: providentiality. The three are made into a square. In the critical literature, providentiality is interpreted as a fourth stage, as that point at which civil order falls completely apart at the end of a *corso* or *ricorso*. Vico regards this point of chaos not as a separate age but as an end that is also a beginning. He does regard this termination of the third age of the *corso* and the beginning of the first age of the *ricorso* as governed by providence. But the sequence of *corso e ricorso* is governed by providence. It is what providence is, the divine order of history. In what sense can there be a separate fourth age that is an age of providence?

Vico's three ages are Dante's terza rima writ large. Three is the logic of advancing time. Four closes time. The *Divine Comedy*, like *Finnegans Wake*, is a circle. As he exits Paradiso, Dante finds himself back in the world where he started, but wiser for his journey, just as Aeneas does through the agency of his golden bough. The motion of the heavenly spheres and the divine is the circle; the circle is the perfect figure. Providentiality as the fourth corner of the square brings with it the circle. It suggests the double circling of the square as diagonal in the geometry lesson of the classbook section of the *Wake* shows (293). Providentiality is a unique fourth age because it is not an age at all; it is what is already in the three ages—as what is ideal in them.

Vico explains that this eternal historical pattern is ideal because the actual course of any nation is only approximate in its detail to this pattern. But the pattern is itself real, not ideal in the sense of an abstract standard. It is IDEAREAL. Providentiality is the corner from which the square can be circled. The circle must have a locus point in the square in order that it is not simply imposed on it externally. There must be a point, so to speak, at which the contraries are coincident—that there is an equal of opposites, as Bruno, following Cusanus, has instructed. By making providence a part of the square Joyce brings the divine into history's commodious recirculation and takes it out of Vico's hands, as the Christian God is transcendent of history, yet directs it.

Providence resides within us, within our memory as our ability to enact coincidences without this process simply becoming chaos. *Finnegans Wake* is not chaos, not non-sense but a cosmos: "every person, place and thing in the chaosmos of Alle anyway connected with the gobblydumped turkey was moving and changing every part of the time. . . . as time went on as it will variously inflected, differently pronounced, otherwise spelled, changeably meaning vocable scriptsigns" (118.21–28).

It is the nature of the words with their given meanings that keeps us from memory simply being a descent into the chaotic. Within memory, as Vico says, is ingenuity (*ingegno*, *ingenium*), which puts things into order while giving them a new turn. Providence is within memory as its function as ingenuity of constantly finding the similar in some sense in the dissimilar. To the pun as Joyce's master key we may add a second key: the idea of circling the square.

Finnegans Wake is divided into four parts, the last corresponding to providentiality. Fours, a pair of pairs, echo throughout the *Wake*. In the fourth book, all of Joyce's themes concerning Vico are capsulized in a single paragraph that is also a single sentence, prefaced by the combination "Forget, remember!"

> Our wholemole millwheeling vicociclometer, a tetradomational gazebocroticon (the "Mamma Lujah" known to every schoolboy scandaller, be he Matty, Marky, Lukey or John-a-Donk), autokinatonetically preprovided with a clappercoupling smeltingworks exprogressive process, (for the farmer, his son and their homely codes, known as eggburst, eggblend, eggburial and hatch-as-hatch can) receives through a portal vein the dialytically separated elements of precedent decomposition for the verypetpurpose of subsequent recombination so that the heroticisms, catastrophes and eccentricities transmitted by the ancient legacy of the past, type by tope, letter from litter, word at ward, with sendence of sundance, since the days of Plooney and Columcellas when Giacinta, Pervenche and Margaret swayed over the all-too-ghoulish and illyrical and innumantic in our mutter nation, all, anastomosically assimilated and preteridentified paraidiotically, in fact, the sameold gamebold adomic structure of

> our Finnius the old One, as highly charged with electrons as hophazards can effective it, may be there for you, Cockalooralooraloomenos, when cup, platter and pot come piping hot, as sure as herself pits hen to paper and there's scribings scrawled on eggs. (614.27–615.10)

The four authors of the "Mamalujo" (397.03, 11) are joined with Joyce's four-term transformation of Vico's three ages, and this is joined with Joyce's fourth but partial parody of Quinet's passage on the cycles of history, which is joined with the theme of the hen who first creates literature by scratching up a letter from litter, in the early part of the work. History is the great "Dirtdump" (615.12) from which all that is in memory is returned, "being humus the same roturns. He who runes may rede it on all fours" (18.05–6). This includes the coursings and recoursings of the identities of Shem and Shaun—Cain and Abel, Shem and Ham, "Yem or Yan" (yin and yang) (246.31). As Joyce plays on H. C. E. and Earwicker, and thus the figure of Vico, all the way through *Finnegans Wake*, so he plays, on page after page, on the combination of the four ages: "Four things therefore, saith our herodotary Mammon Lujius in his grand old historiorum" (13.20–21).

What more is there to be said? We have arrived at "the last of the first" (111.10). The *Wake* does not last forever. The philosophers return to their places in history. Forget, remember! We are always forgetting. As Hegel states in the *Phenomenology of Spirit*, consciousness always forgets and must begin again from the beginning. The wisdom of philosophy, the love of wisdom, is that it acts against forgetting. It is always reconstructing, resurrecting the whole, which Vico says is "really the flower of wisdom." Philosophy, at least speculative philosophy, has this commitment to reason. Joyce keeps us from forgetting through his commitment to imagination as memory. Philosophy only arises and only is of use when we find ourselves among barbarians. It is then we need to remember.

We come upon the riverrun of *Finnegans Wake* with its naming of Eve and Adam and Vico and Bruno, its doubling of Dublin on the Oconee, its thunder word, and the Humpty Dumpty fall of Finnegan "erse solid man," the first stolid man, and Livy the historian and the Liffey. And we ask ourselves: why did Joyce write it, where is Joyce taking us, and why, *unde et ubi*? If history is a nightmare from which we are trying to awake, we will understand. If not, we are better off as we are—as Plato says, most are asleep.

Homer recounts episodes of the Trojan War and the wanderings of Odysseus, and in so doing brings the past into the present and invents history. Dante, in the middle of his life's journey, brings forth the eternal present of the other world of the Inferno, Purgatorio, and Paradiso, the future that transcends history, into his and our present. Joyce, instead of awakening us to take us beyond history, puts us to sleep within it. We enter history in a conscious dream in which we wander with Joyce as our Virgil.

We master history, not by awakening from its progressive order of advancing ages, one causally related to the next, but by dreaming it while fully awake. The nightmare of history depends upon our taking history seriously. Instead we are instructed by Joyce, the Irish clown, how not to be serious. Croce says that Vico "looks at history and never smiles." Joyce does nothing but smile. Yet this lack of the serious is not simple comedy. It is irony. The puns of Shem the penman are ironic. They make words mean other and opposite than they do as ordinary terms. Irony, by being a refusal to state the literal, allows us to see, hear, and feel something more, something that is beyond language.

Joyce's readers are of a different purpose than Joyce's critics. The critics see the *Wake* as a giant puzzle to be put together. The readers are seated on the other side of the room. We readers are like Joyce late at night, as Nora reported, chuckling to ourselves as we reorder history through its coincidences and cycles, turning the pages, finding relief from the literal truth by facing its double truth.

And, if philosophy must continually go to school with the poets to overcome Plato's quarrel, Joyce, the greatest writer of modern times, has kept the school doors open. We have only to enter and mind our boots goan in.

Appendix

✦

Register of Philosophers at the Wake

The following are sixty-five philosophers present at the Wake. Each entry is accompanied by citations selected from Adaline Glasheen's *Third Census of "Finnegans Wake."* They appear here chronologically by date of birth. Several associates of philosophy are included, such as Darwin, Freud, and Einstein, as they have had significant influence on philosophy.

Pythagoras (c. 570–c. 495 B.C.) 116.30
Anaxagoras (c. 500–428 B.C.) 155.32–33
Socrates (469–399 B.C.) 88.09; 306.L11
Democritus (c. 460–c. 370 B.C.) 551.31
Plato (427–347 B.C.) 119.03; 164.11; 257.11; 286.03; 292.30; 307.L01; 348.08; 417.15; 622.36
Diogenes (c. 400–c. 325 B.C.) 184.17; 290.21; 307.L05; 411.29; 421.26
Aristotle (384–322 B.C.) 110.17; 306.L05; 417.16
Epicurus (341–271 B.C.) 475.11
Cicero (106–43 B.C.) 152.10; 182.09; 425.19; 577.28
Lucretius (c. 99–55 B.C.) 277n2; 306.L16
Seneca, the Younger (c. 1–65) 612.15
Lucian (c. 115–c. 200) 255.21; 419.36
Marcus Aurelius (121–80) 132.19; 306.L14
Plotinus (204–70) 470.20
Porphyry (233–304) 264n3
Augustine, Saint (354–430) 38.29–30
Pelagius (c. 354–c. 425) 182.03; 358.10; 387.05–6; 525.C7; 538.36
Eriugena, John Scotus (c. 810–77) 4.36; 279.03; 431.21, 35
Avicenna (980–1037) 488.06–7, 15
Abelard, Peter (1079–1144) 237.34–35; 453.26
Averroës (1126–98) 488.07, 15
Bonaventure, Saint (c. 1221–74) 207.26
Aquinas, Saint Thomas (1225–74) 93.09; 113.36; 145.10; 240.08; 245.12; 296.20; 299.08; 417.08; 510.18; 514.17
Nicholas of Cusa (1401–64) 16.05; 49.34; 85.30; 163.15, 17; 518.23; 622.01
Erasmus, Desiderius (1466–1536) 155.33; 301n5
Machiavelli, Niccolò (1469–1527) 89.06–7; 182.20; 251.26–27

NOTES

Introduction

1. Plato, *The Republic of Plato*, trans. Allan Bloom (New York: Basic Books, 1991), 70.

2. Ibid., 72.

3. Ibid., 76.

4. Richard Ellmann, *James Joyce*, rev. ed. (New York: Oxford University Press, 1982), 103n.

5. Ibid., 118, 512.

6. James Joyce, *Ulysses*, ed. Hans Walter Gabler (New York: Vintage, 1986), 153.

7. Plato, *Republic*, 291.

8. Ibid.

9. Ibid., 290.

10. Hesiod, *Theogony*, trans. Norman O. Brown (Indianapolis, Ind.: Bobbs-Merrill, 1953), 53.

11. "Filofol" and "saige-fol" are Rabelaisian. See Roland McHugh, *Annotations to Finnegans Wake*, rev. ed. (Baltimore: Johns Hopkins University Press, 1991), 119.

12. Letter to Harriet Shaw Weaver (March 26, 1928), in *Selected Letters of James Joyce,* ed. Richard Ellmann (New York: Viking, 1992), 331.

13. Plato, *Epistle VII*, in vol. 9 of *Plato*, trans. R. G. Bury (Cambridge, Mass.: Harvard University Press, 1989), 533.

14. Plato, *Timaeus*, in vol. 9 of *Plato*, 53 (29b).

15. Ernst Cassirer, *The Problem of Knowledge: Philosophy, Science, and History Since Hegel*, trans. William H. Woglom and Charles W. Hendel (New Haven, Conn.: Yale University Press, 1950), 296.

16. Ernst Cassirer, *Language and Myth*, trans. Susanne K. Langer (New York: Dover, 1946), 98–99.

17. Postcard to Harriet Shaw Weaver (April 16, 1927), in Ellmann, ed., *Selected Letters*, 321.

18. Aristotle, *Parts of Animals*, trans. W. Ogle, in *The Complete Works of Aristotle*, ed. Jonathan Barnes, 2 vols. (Princeton, N.J.: Princeton University Press, 1984), 1:1049.

19. Ellmann, *Joyce*, 693.

20. For these comments, see ibid., 703.

21. Ellmann, ed., *Selected Letters*, 316. This letter, as it appeared in *Letters of James Joyce,* ed. Stuart Gilbert (New York: Viking, 1957), 247, has "Jeems Joker" as Joyce's internal signature. I presume this is an error and that "Jeems Jokes" is correct to the original, in accord with Ellmann's statement in the "Preface" that letters from the Gilbert volume "have been retranscribed whenever possible" (viii). "Jokes" preserves Joyce's pun better than "Joker."

22. Plato, *Laws*, in *Complete Works*, ed. John M. Cooper (Indianapolis, Ind.: Hackett, 1997), 1420.

23. Giambattista Vico, *On the Most Ancient Wisdom of the Italians*, trans. Jason Taylor (New Haven, Conn.: Yale University Press, 2010), chap. 1.

24. Heinrich Straumann, "Last Meeting with Joyce," in *A James Joyce Yearbook*, ed. Maria Jolas (Paris: Transition, 1949), 114.

25. Letter to Harriet Shaw Weaver (November 15, 1926), in Ellmann, ed., *Selected Letters*, 316.

26. Ellmann, *Joyce*, 583n.

27. Louis Gillet, *Claybook for James Joyce*, trans. Georges Markow-Totevy (London: Abelard-Schuman, 1958), 66.

Chapter 1

1. Letter to Harriet Shaw Weaver (May 21, 1926), in Ellmann, ed., *Selected Letters*, 314.

2. Adaline Glasheen, *Third Census of "Finnegans Wake": An Index of the Characters and Their Roles*, rev. ed. (Berkeley: University of California Press, 1977), 298.

3. The abridged edition is *The New Science of Giambattista Vico*, trans. Thomas Goddard Bergin and Max Harold Fisch, rev. and abbrev. (Ithaca, N.Y.: Cornell University Press, 1970), originally published as a Doubleday Anchor paperback in 1961. As the translators state in their preface: "we have reduced the bulk of Vico's text by about one third" (xiv).

4. Ellmann, *Joyce*, 59–60.

5. Domenico Pietropaolo, "Vico and Literary History in the Early Joyce," in *Vico and Joyce*, ed. Donald Phillip Verene (Albany: State University of New York Press, 1987), 102.

6. C. P. Curran, *James Joyce Remembered* (London: Oxford University Press, 1968), 121.

7. James Joyce, "James Clarence Mangan," in *The Critical Writings of James Joyce*, ed. Ellsworth Mason and Richard Ellmann (Ithaca, N.Y.: Cornell University Press, 1989), 81–83. The editors regard the source of these remarks as theosophy, perhaps coming to Joyce through Yeats.

8. Joyce resided in via Donato Bramante from September 15, 1912 to June 18, 1915.

9. Ellmann, *Joyce*, 340.

10. Ibid., 340n.

11. James Joyce, "Vico (Cornell)," in *Notes, Criticism, Translations, and Miscellaneous Writings: A Facsimile of Manuscripts and Typescripts*, vol. 2, ed. Hans Walter Gabler, in *The James Joyce Archive* (New York: Garland, 1979), 391–93. The typescript is identified as "Trieste or Zurich years" (1905–20). See also Andrew Treip, "The Cornell Notes on Vico," *La Revue des lettres modernes: James Joyce 3, Joyce et l'Italie*, ed. Claude Jacquet and Jean-Michel Rabaté (Paris: Lettres Modernes, 1994), 217–20.

12. See Joyce's comment to Harriet Shaw Weaver on this passage from Quinet in Ellmann, ed., *Selected Letters*, 355.

13. Ellmann, *Joyce*, 664.

14. Mary and Padraic Colum, *Our Friend James Joyce* (Gloucester, Mass.: Peter Smith, 1968; 1958), 81.

15. Curran, *Joyce Remembered*, 86–87. The passage Joyce pointed out to Curran combines lines from Michelet's "Avant-propos" and his introduction, "Discours sur le systèm et la vie de Vico," to *Oeuvres choisies de Vico* (1835). See Jules Michelet, *Oeuvres complètes*, vol. 1, ed. Paul Viallaneix (Paris: Flammarion, 1971), 281, 287–88.

16. Ellmann, ed., *Selected Letters*, 321.

17. Ellmann, *Joyce*, 564.

18. Ellmann, ed., *Selected Letters*, 317.

19. Stuart Gilbert, ed., *Letters of James Joyce* (New York: Viking, 1957), 204. The annalists to whom Joyce refers are the Franciscan monks who compiled the *Annals of the Four Masters*, written between 1632 and 1636, giving the history of Ireland; they appear as figures in *Finnegans Wake* and can be associated with the four Evangelists (256.21).

20. Hegel's omission of a stage of mythical consciousness in the *Phenomenology of Spirit* is a criticism advanced by Ernst Cassirer. For an account of this, see Donald Phillip Verene, *The Origins of the Philosophy of Symbolic Forms: Kant, Hegel, and Cassirer* (Evanston, Ill.: Northwestern University Press, 2011), chap. 2.

21. Benedetto Croce, "An Unknown Page from the Last Months of Hegel's Life," trans. James W. Hillesheim and Ernesto Caserta, *New Vico Studies* 26 (2008): 143–65.

22. Colum, *Our Friend James Joyce*, 82.

23. Richard Ellmann, ed., *Letters of James Joyce,* vol. 3 (New York: Viking, 1966), 117–18.

24. Ibid., 480.

25. H. P. Adams, *The Life and Writings of Giambattista Vico* (London: Allen and Unwin, 1935); Robert Flint, *Vico* (Edinburgh: Blackwood, 1884).

26. Jacques Mercanton, "The Hours of James Joyce," in *Portraits of the Artist in Exile: Recollections of James Joyce by Europeans*, ed. Willard Potts (New York: Harcourt Brace Jovanovich, 1986), 207.

27. Ellmann, ed., *Letters*, 3:463.

28. Heinrich Straumann, "Last Meeting with Joyce," in *A James Joyce Yearbook*, ed. Maria Jolas (Paris: Transition, 1949), 114.

29. Samuel Beckett, "Dante . . . Bruno. Vico . . Joyce," in *Our Exagmination Round His Factification for Incamination of Work in Progress* (Norfolk, Conn.: New Directions, 1962; 1929), 1–22.

30. Anthony Burgess, ed., *A Shorter Finnegans Wake* (New York: Viking, 1968), xiii.

31. H. S. Harris, "What is Mr. Ear-Vico Supposed to be 'Earing'?" in *Vico and Joyce*, ed. Donald Phillip Verene (Albany: State University of New York Press, 1987), 72. An exception to Harris's claim is the chapter on Vico in John Bishop, *Joyce's Book of the Dark: Finnegans Wake* (Madison: University of Wisconsin Press, 1986). Bishop's book appeared after the conference in June 1985 at which Harris's paper was presented.

32. Ellmann, ed., *Selected Letters*, 344.

33. James Joyce, *A Portrait of the Artist as a Young Man*, ed. Seamus Deane (New York: Penguin, 1993), 271; compare *Stephen Hero* (New York: New Directions, 1944), 170.

34. Adolph Hoffmeister, "Portrait of Joyce," in *Portraits*, ed. Potts, 129. See also Beckett, "Dante . . . ," 21.

35. Colum, *Our Friend James Joyce*, 124.

36. Beckett, "Dante . . . ," 4.

37. Benedetto Croce, *La filosofia di Giambattista Vico* (Bari: Laterza, 1965; 1911). Beckett could also have consulted Robert Flint's *Vico*, which appeared as a volume of the series "Philosophical Classics for English Readers." The interpretation in it would have been more to Beckett's liking; perhaps he did not know of it.

38. Croce, *La filosofia*, 77 (my translation).

39. See Hegel's *Vorrede* in *Phänomenologie des Geistes*, ed. Johannes Hoffmeister, 6th ed. (Hamburg: Meiner, 1952). On the difference between speculation and reflection, see Donald Phillip Verene, *Hegel's Absolute: An Introduction to Reading the "Phenomenology of Spirit"* (Albany: State University of New York Press, 2007), chap. 1.

40. Joyce, *A Portrait*, 271.

41. Colum, *Our Friend James Joyce*, 82. Andrea Battistini, "Beckett e Vico," *Bollettino del Centro di Studi Vichiani* 5 (1975), regards "roundheaded" as *coined* by Joyce: "Riecheggiando persino degli stilemi tipicamente joyciani per i loro fantastici accostamenti—si pensi soltano alla definizione del Vico come 'una specie di "testa tonda," di puritano partenopeo,' del tutto identica a quella coniata da Joyce" (79).

42. Ruth Dudley Edwards, *Matricide at St. Martha's* (New York: St. Martin's, 1995), 167.

43. Beckett, "Dante . . . ," 5.

44. See *Principj di Scienza Nuova d'intorno alla Comune Natura delle Nazioni: Corcordanze e indici di frequenza dell'edizione Napoli 1744*, ed. Marco Veneziani (Florence: Olschki, 1997), 629–30.

45. Croce, *La filosofia*, 113.

46. Ibid., 223.

47. Beckett claims ("Dante . . . ," 4) that Vico derived his three ages from the report of Herodotus that the Egyptians had three kinds of writing (*Hist.* 2.36). Vico mentions this but is clear that his principal source is Varro's view of three ages, found in the odd little book of Censorinus, *De die natali*, sec. 21.

48. Beckett, "Dante . . . ," 8.

49. Ibid., 5.

50. Ibid., 5–6.

51. Liselotte Dieckmann, "Giambattista Vico's Use of 'Renaissance Hieroglyphics,'" *Forum Italicum* 2 (1968): 385.

52. Mary T. Reynolds, *Joyce and Dante: The Shaping Imagination* (Princeton, N.J.: Princeton University Press, 1981), 207.

53. Beckett, "Dante . . . ," 18–19.

54. Reynolds, *Joyce and Dante*, 203.

55. Ibid., 203–4.

56. Charles S. Singleton, "Commentary," in Dante Alighieri, *The Divine Comedy: Inferno*, trans. Charles S. Singleton (Princeton, N.J.: Princeton University Press, 1970), 108–9.

57. See the commentary on this passage in Giambattista Vico, *Opere*, ed. Andrea Battistini, 2 vols. (Milan: Mondadori, 1990), 2:1591n10.

58. Reynolds, *Joyce and Dante*, 6.

59. Ibid., 214.

60. Charles S. Singleton, "Commentary," in Dante Alighieri, *The Divine Comedy: Paradiso*, 574.

61. Ellmann, ed., *Selected Letters*, 321.

62. Umberto Eco, *The Aesthetics of Chaosmos: The Middle Ages of James Joyce*, trans. Ellen Esrock (Cambridge, Mass.: Harvard University Press, 1989), 75.

63. Ibid., 75–76.

64. Beckett, "Dante . . . ," 19.

65. Eco, *Aesthetics of Chaosmos*, 64.

66. Umberto Eco, *The Name of the Rose*, trans. William Weaver (New York: Harcourt Brace Jovanovich, 1983), 46–47.

67. Ibid., 425.

68. Ibid., 491.

69. George Santayana, *Three Philosophical Poets*, vol. 6 of *The Works of George Santayana*, Triton Edition (New York: Scribner's, 1936), 84.

70. Ellmann, *Joyce*, 340, 342.

71. Ellmann, ed., *Letters*, 3:166.

72. Eco, *Aesthetics of Chaosmos*, 82.

73. Giambattista Vico, "Dante's 'Barbarousness'; Three Reasons for Reading Him, 1725, 1728–9," in *Dante: The Critical Heritage 1314(?)–1870*, ed. Michael Caesar (New York: Routledge, 1989), 352.

74. Ibid., 351–52.

75. Eco, *Aesthetics of Chaosmos*, 83–84.

Chapter 2

1. Thornton Wilder, *The Skin of Our Teeth*, in *Three Plays* (New York: Harper Perennial, 2006), 219. On *Finnegans Wake* as the source for Wilder's play, see the "Afterword" by Tappan Wilder, 449–56. See also "The Wilder Affair," in Joseph Campbell, *Mythic Worlds, Modern Words: On the Art of James Joyce*, ed. Edmund L. Epstein (Novato, Calif.: New World Library, 1993), 257–67.
Regarding Wilder's interest in *Finnegans Wake*, see E. M. Burns and J. A. Gaylord, *A Tour of the Darkling Plain: The Finnegans Wake Letters of Thornton Wilder and Adaline Glasheen* (Dublin: University College, 2001). Glasheen often cites the view of "Mr. Wilder" in entries of her *Third Census*.

2. G. S. Kirk and J. E. Raven, *The Presocratic Philosophers: A Critical History with a Selection of Texts* (Cambridge: Cambridge University Press, 1966), 376.

3. Ibid., 365.

4. Plato, *The Last Days of Socrates: Euthyphro, Apology, Crito, Phaedo*, trans. Hugh Tredennick and Harold Tarrant (New York: Penguin, 1969), 161.

5. J. W. von Goethe, *Gedenkausgabe der Werke, Briefe und Gespräche*, 24 vols., ed. Ernst Beuther, *Naturwissenschaftliche Schriften, Erster Teil* (Zurich: Artemis-Verlag, 1949), 16:346–47 (my translation).

6. Cicero, *De oratore*, trans. H. Rackham (Cambridge, Mass.: Harvard University Press, 2004), bk. 3, 109.

7. John Scotus Eriugena, *On the Division of Nature*, in *Medieval Philosophy: From St. Augustine to Nicholas of Cusa*, ed. John F. Wippel and Allan B. Wolter (New York: Free Press, 1969), 113.

8. James Joyce, *Ulysses*, ed. Hans Walter Gabler (New York: Vintage, 1986), 39.

9. Niccolò Machiavelli, *The Prince*, in *Machiavelli: The Chief Works and Others*, 3 vols., trans. Allan Gilbert (Durham, N.C.: Duke University Press, 1989), 1:57.

10. Dante Alighieri, *The Divine Comedy: Inferno*, trans. Charles S. Singleton (Princeton, N.J.: Princeton University Press, 1970), 5.

11. Ibid., 7.

12. Galileo Galilei, *The Starry Messenger*, in *Discoveries and Opinions of Galileo*, trans. Stillman Drake (New York: Doubleday, 1957), 46.

13. Machiavelli, *Works*, 2:929.

14. Dante, *Inferno*, commentary on canto 5, 94–95.

15. Francis Bacon, *Novum Organum*, in *The Works of Francis Bacon*, ed. James Spedding, Robert Leslie Ellis, and Douglas Denon Heath, vol. 4 (New York: Garrett, 1968), 47.

16. René Descartes, *Meditations on First Philosophy*, in *The Philosophical Writings of Descartes*, 3 vols., trans. John Cottingham, Robert Stoothoff, Dugald Murdoch, and Anthony Kenny (Cambridge: Cambridge University Press, 1991), 2:14.

17. Ibid., 2:19.

18. Ibid., 3:159.

19. Giambattista Vico, *On the Most Ancient Wisdom of the Italians*, trans. Jason Taylor (New Haven, Conn.: Yale University Press, 2000), 33.

20. Descartes, "Early Writings," in *Writings*, 1:2.

21. Descartes, *Discourse on the Method*, in *Writings*, 1:111.

22. George Berkeley, *Philosophical Commentaries*, in *The Works of George Berkeley, Bishop of Cloyne*, ed. A. A. Luce and T. E. Jessop, 9 vols. (Edinburgh: Thomas Nelson, 1948–57), 1: entry 392.

23. George Berkeley, *Three Dialogues between Hylas and Philonous*, ed. Robert Merrihew Adams (Indianapolis, Ind.: Hackett, 1986), 3.

24. The critical edition of *Finnegans Wake* by Rose and O'Hanlon (see "Bibliographical Note" herein) gives these variations on Berkeley's name: "the Burkeley bump" (*FW* 2, 240.40), compare "the Burklley bump" (312.29), and "Belkelly" (*FW* 2, 478.02), compare "Balkelly" (611.05).

25. Immanuel Kant, *Critique of Pure Reason*, trans. Norman Kemp Smith (London: Macmillan, 1958), 9n.

26. Hegel's dialectic, characterized as thesis-antithesis-synthesis, as is popularly held, is incorrect. He never employs such a characterization, and in fact, attributes "triplicity" to the false method of Kant. See Donald Phillip Verene, "The Double *Ansich*," chapter 2 of *Hegel's Absolute: An Introduction to Reading the "Phenomenology of Spirit"* (Albany: State University of New York Press, 2007).

27. Bertolt Brecht, *Flüchtlingsgespräche* (Berlin: Suhrkamp, 1961), 108–11 (my translation).

28. The words "very priveetly, of course, to" and the parentheses appear in the critical edition of Rose and O'Hanlon (see "Bibliographical Note" herein), but not in the original edition of 1939.

29. Donald Phillip Verene, "Coincidence, Historical Repetition, and Self-Knowledge: Jung, Vico, and Joyce," *Journal of Analytical Psychology* 47 (2002):

459–78. Reprinted in *Synchronicity: Multiple Perspectives on Meaningful Coincidence*, ed. Lance Storm, School of Psychology, Adelaide (Siena: Pari, 2008).

30. Donald Phillip Verene, "Freud's Consulting Room Archeology and Vico's Principles of Humanity," *British Journal of Psychotherapy* 13 (1997): 499–505. Reprinted in electronic format by Artesian Books (2006).

31. Richard Ellmann, ed., *Selected Letters of James Joyce* (London: Faber and Faber, 1975), 282.

32. Sigmund Freud, *Jokes and Their Relation to the Unconscious*, vol. 8 of *The Standard Edition of the Complete Psychological Works of Sigmund Freud*, trans. James Strachey and Anna Freud (London: Hogarth Press and the Institute of Psycho-Analysis, 1960), 45.

33. Ellmann, ed., *Letters,* 3:262.

34. Ellmann, *Joyce*, 628.

35. G. W. F. Hegel, *Phenomenology of Spirit*, trans. A. V. Miller (New York: Oxford University Press, 1977), 205.

Chapter 3

1. Adaline Glasheen, *Third Census of "Finnegans Wake": An Index of the Characters and Their Roles* (Berkeley: University of California Press, 1977), 206 and 262 (see entry on Shem).

2. J. Lewis McIntyre, *Giordano Bruno* (London: Macmillan, 1903), 142–48; James Joyce, "The Bruno Philosophy," in *The Critical Writings of James Joyce*, ed. Ellsworth Mason and Richard Ellmann (New York: Viking, 1959), 132–34.

3. Giordano Bruno, *On the Infinite Universe and Worlds*, in Dorothea Waley Singer, *Giordano Bruno: His Life and Thought* (New York: Schuman, 1950), 307.

4. Giordano Bruno, *Cause, Principle and Unity*, trans. Robert de Lucca (Cambridge: Cambridge University Press, 1998), 96–97.

5. Giordano Bruno, *The Expulsion of the Triumphant Beast*, trans. Arthur D. Imerti (Lincoln: University of Nebraska Press, 1964), 221.

6. Ibid., 304n8. See also David Eugene Smith, *A Source Book in Mathematics* (New York: Dover, 1959; 1929), 99.

7. This thesis is most fully developed by Ernst Cassirer, *Das Erkenntnisproblem in der Philosophie und Wissenschaft der neueren Zeit*, vol. 1 (Hamburg: Meiner, 1999; 1906), chap. 1. See also Ernst Cassirer, *The Individual and the Cosmos in Renaissance Philosophy*, trans. Mario Domandi (New York: Harper and Row, 1964), chap. 1.

8. Ernst Cassirer, "The Influence of Language upon the Development of Scientific Thought," *Journal of Philosophy* 39 (1942): 309–27.

9. Ovid, *Metamorphoses*, trans. Frank Justus Miller (Cambridge, Mass.: Harvard University Press, 2004), 3–5 (1.21–23).

10. Nicholas of Cusa, *De docta ignorantia*, in *Complete Philosophical and Theological Treatises of Nicholas of Cusa*, vol. 1, trans. Jasper Hopkins (Minneapolis, Minn.: Arthur J. Banning, 2001), 20.

11. See Beckett, "Dante . . . ," 17.

12. I. Frith, *Life of Giordano Bruno the Nolan* (London: Trübner, 1887), reprinted: Adamant Media, 2007.

13. Beckett, "Dante . . . ," 17. Joyce, "Day of the Rabblement," 69. The line as it appears in Frith, *Life*, is: "'No man truly loves goodness and truth who is not incensed with the multitude'" (165). Frith cites this quotation as coming from an edition of Bruno's works containing *Gli eroici furori* and some sonnets (323).

14. Ellmann, *Joyce*, 89 and note. Ibsen's line is "At leve er—krig med trolde." See M. C. Bradbrook, *Ibsen the Norwegian: A Revaluation* (Hamden, Conn.: Archon, 1966), 16.

15. Stuart Gilbert, ed. *Letters of James Joyce* (New York: Viking, 1957), 224–25.

16. Bruno, *Infinite Universe*, 369.

17. Bruno, *Cause*, 66.

18. For an account of Bruno's expansion of Copernicus, see Antoinette Mann Paterson, *The Infinite Worlds of Giordano Bruno* (Springfield, Ill.: Charles C. Thomas, 1970), chap. 1.

19. Giordano Bruno, *The Ash Wednesday Supper*, ed. and trans. Edward A. Gosselin and Lawrence S. Lerner (Toronto: University of Toronto Press, 1995), 155.

20. Bruno, *Infinite Universe*, 266–67.

21. Stanislaus Joyce, *My Brother's Keeper: James Joyce's Early Years*, ed. Richard Ellmann (New York: Viking, 1959), 121.

22. See Singer's commentary in *Bruno*, 179n79; see also McIntyre, *Bruno*, 95.

23. Bruno, *Triumphant Beast*, 74.

24. Ibid., 79.

25. Thomas Aquinas, *The Disputed Questions on Truth*, 3 vols., trans. Robert W. Mulligan (Chicago: Regnery, 1953), 2:319–20.

26. Bruno, *Triumphant Beast*, 80.

27. Ibid., 90–91.

28. Singer, *Bruno*, 120. On Bruno and the Cabala, see Frances A. Yates, *Giordano Bruno and the Hermetic Tradition* (Chicago: University of Chicago Press, 1991), chap. 14.

29. Quoted in Karen Silvia de Léon-Jones, *Giordano Bruno and the Kabbalah: Prophets, Magicians, and Rabbis* (Lincoln: University of Nebraska Press, 2004), 117.

30. Giordano Bruno, *The Heroic Enthusiasts*, trans. L. Williams (London: George Redway, 1887), 58, reprinted by Kessinger Publishing, n.d.

31. Ibid., 61.

32. Bruno, *Triumphant Beast*, 80.

33. Bruno, *Heroic*, 131–32.

34. Plato, *Cratylus*, trans. C. D. C. Reeve, in *Complete Works*, ed. John M. Cooper (Indianapolis, Ind.: Hackett, 1997), 117 (398d).

35. Glasheen, *Third Census*, 206, 262.

36. Jacques Mercanton, "The Hours of James Joyce," in *Portraits of the Artist in Exile: Recollections of James Joyce by Europeans*, ed. Willard Potts (New York: Harcourt Brace Jovanovich, 1986), 213.

37. Joyce, *Ulysses*, 20.

38. Jorge Luis Borges, "The Immortal," in *Collected Fictions*, trans. Andrew Hurley (New York: Penguin, 1998), 183.

Chapter 4

1. John Bishop, *Joyce's Book of the Dark: Finnegans Wake* (Madison: University of Wisconsin Press, 1986), 174.

2. Ibid., 175–76. See Ellmann, *Joyce*, 340.

3. Jorge Luis Borges, *This Craft of Verse*, ed. Calin-Andrei Mihailescu (Cambridge, Mass.: Harvard University Press, 2000), 88–89.

4. Sir John Harington (1560–1612) designed the modern indoor water closet in his work *A New Discourse of a Stale Subject, Called the Metamorphosis of Ajax*, crit. ed. Elizabeth Strong Donno (New York: Columbia University Press; London: Routledge and Kegan Paul, 1962). See the materials list and design, 194–96. "This is Don A Jax house, of the new fashion," 195 ("jakes," from the French *Jacques* [James], "privy"). "Ajaculate! [Ajax, a jakes, ejaculate]" (338.17).

5. Giambattista Vico, *The Autobiography of Giambattista Vico*, trans. Max Harold Fisch and Thomas Goddard Bergin (Ithaca, N.Y.: Cornell University Press, 1975), 111; Giambattista Vico, *Vita di Giambattista Vico scritta da se medesimo*, in *Opere*, ed. Andrea Battistini, 2 vols. (Milan: Mondadori, 1990), 1:5 (my translation).

6. Joseph Campbell, *Mythic Worlds, Modern Words: On the Art of James Joyce*, ed. Edmund L. Epstein (Novato, Calif.: New World Library, 1993), 208.

7. See Adaline Glasheen, *Third Census of "Finnegans Wake": An Index of the Characters and Their Roles* (Berkeley: University of California Press, 1977), for a text of the Ballad (93).

8. For a full account of Vico's alteration of his birth date, see Donald Phillip Verene, *The New Art of Autobiography: An Essay on the Life of Giambattista Vico Written by Himself* (Oxford: Clarendon, 1991), chap. 5.

9. Ellmann, *Joyce*, 583 and note. From the *Rand McNally Road Atlas* and *U.S. Postal Zip-Code Directory*, I find there are not three but ten Dublins in the United States. I suspect that these likely existed in the 1920s when Joyce made his request of Levy. In the *Wake* there is also "dub gulch" (254.17). Dublin Gulch is a locality in Silver Bow County, near Butte, Montana. See Louis O. Mink, *A Finnegans Wake Gazetteer* (Bloomington: Indiana University Press, 1978), 298.

10. Campbell, *Mythic Worlds*, 206.

11. Vico, *Autobiography*, 111; *Vita*, 5 (my translation).

12. For an account of the practice of the use of historical dates by ancient historians, see A. Dreizehnter, *Die rhetorische Zahl: Quellenkritische Untersuchungen anhand der Zahlen 70 und 700* (Munich: Beck, 1978).

13. Giambattista Vico, *L'autobiografia, il carteggio e le poesie varie*, in vol. 5 of *Opere di G. B. Vico*, ed. B. Croce and F. Nicolini, 2nd rev. ed. (Bari: Laterza, 1929), 377.

14. Giambattista Vico, "The Academies and the Relation between Philosophy and Eloquence," trans. Donald Phillip Verene, in Giambattista Vico, *On the Study Methods of Our Time*, trans. Elio Gianturco (Ithaca, N.Y.: Cornell University Press, 1990), 90.

15. For the coining of the term "autobiography," see Verene, *New Art of Autobiography*, 53–54.

16. Vico, *Autobiography*, 182.

17. Ibid., v.

18. Ibid., 182.

19. Ibid., 113.

20. René Descartes, *Discourse on the Method*, in *The Philosophical Writings of Descartes*, 3 vols., trans. John Cottingham, Robert Stoothoff, Dugald Murdoch, and Anthony Kenny (Cambridge: Cambridge University Press, 1991), 2:114–15.

21. Vico, *Autobiography*, 113.

22. Augustine, *City of God*, trans. David S. Wiesen, vol. 3 (Cambridge, Mass.: Harvard University Press, 1968), 555 (9.31).

23. Vico, *Autobiography*, 132.

24. Ibid., 133.

25. Giambattista Vico, "Vindication of Vico," trans. Donald Phillip Verene, in *Giambattista Vico: Keys to the New Science; Translations, Commentaries, and Essays*, ed. Thora Ilin Bayer and Donald Phillip Verene (Ithaca, N.Y.: Cornell University Press, 2009), 109.

26. Gustavo Costa, "Vico e l'Inquisizione," *Nouvelles de la République des Lettres* 2 (1999): 93–124.

27. Giambattista Vico, *On the Most Ancient Wisdom of the Italians*, trans. Jason Taylor (New Haven, Conn.: Yale University Press, 2010), chap. 1.

28. Giambattista Vico, *Epistole con aggiunte le epistole dei suoi corrispondenti*, ed. Manuel Sanna (Naples: Centro di Studi Vichiani, 1992), 114.

29. Richard Berheimer, "Theatrum mundi," *Art Bulletin* 28 (1956): 225–47.

30. Giulio Camillo, *L'idea del theatro*, ed. Lina Bolzoni (Palermo: Sellerio, 1991). See also Frances A. Yates, *The Art of Memory* (Chicago: University of Chicago Press, 1966), chaps. 6 and 7; and Donald Phillip Verene, *Philosophy and the Return to Self-Knowledge* (New Haven, Conn.: Yale University Press, 1997), chap. 4.

31. Paolo Rossi, *Logic and the Art of Memory: The Quest for a Universal Language*, trans. Stephen Clacas (New York: Continuum, 2000), chap. 3.

32. In these lines I have followed the critical edition of Rose and O'Hanlon (see "Bibliographical Note" herein).

33. Anthony Burgess, *Joysprick: An Introduction to the Language of James Joyce* (New York: Harcourt Brace Jovanovich, 1973), 131.

Chapter 5

1. On Bacon's idols, see Donald Phillip Verene, *Vico's Science of Imagination* (Ithaca, N.Y.: Cornell University Press, 1981), chap. 5. See also Donald Phillip Verene, *Vico's New Science: A Philosophical Commentary* (Ithaca, N.Y.: Cornell University Press, 2015).

2. *The Digest of Justinian*, trans. Alan Watson, vol. 1 (Philadelphia: University of Pennsylvania Press, 1985), 1.1.4.

3. The *Digest* defines *ius naturale* differently than that advocated by the seventeenth- and eighteenth-century natural-law theorists. In Roman law *ius naturale* "is not a law specific to mankind but is common to all animals" (1.1.3).

4. Torquato Tasso, *Jerusalem Delivered: Gerusalemme liberata*, trans. Anthony M. Esolen (Baltimore: Johns Hopkins University Press, 2000).

5. In the critical edition of Rose and O'Hanlon (see "Bibliographical Note" herein), these words are given as "Nighty night!" But in his recording of the end of the Anna Livia Plurabelle episode, Joyce, reading these lines, quite clearly

speaks “Night night!” as appears in the 1939 edition. Poetically it is a much stronger expression than “Nighty night!”

6. Jean-Jacques Rousseau, *The First and Second Discourses*, trans. Roger D. Masters and Judith R. Masters (New York: St. Martin’s, 1964), 54.

7. In the critical edition of Rose and O’Hanlon (see “Bibliographical Note” herein), “commodius” of the original 1939 edition is corrected to “commodious.”

INDEX

Appendix entries are not listed here.